William Garden Blaikie

Summer Suns in the Far West

A holiday trip to the Pacific slope

William Garden Blaikie

Summer Suns in the Far West
A holiday trip to the Pacific slope

ISBN/EAN: 9783744754545

Printed in Europe, USA, Canada, Australia, Japan

Cover: Foto ©Andreas Hilbeck / pixelio.de

More available books at **www.hansebooks.com**

Summer Suns

IN THE FAR WEST

A Holiday Trip to the Pacific Slope

BY

W. G. Blaikie, D.D., LL.D.

THOMAS NELSON AND SONS
London, Edinburgh, and New York

1890

Preface.

SOME portions of what follows have already appeared in the form of letters, partly in one journal, partly in another. Many friends, interested in what they read there, have expressed a desire to have a more full and connected record of my tour. I have therefore recast the whole, and added nearly as much as was contained in the original papers, keeping up the style of easy letters, so that the whole might be regarded as written (as much of it was) in the railway carriage. The book is neither more nor less than notes of a holiday trip; and I cannot hope by means of it to do more than enable others to share the information and the pleasure which the trip imparted to the travellers themselves, and perhaps add a little filament to the cord of interest and regard that binds together the two great sections of the Anglo-Saxon family.

Contents.

I. EDINBURGH TO PHILADELPHIA,	9
II. BALTIMORE TO CHICAGO,	22
III. PRAIRIE, AND COLORADO ROCKIES,	33
IV. SALT LAKE CITY AND THE MORMONS,	42
V. THE YOSEMITE VALLEY,	51
VI. LOS ANGELES,	64
VII. SOUTHERN CALIFORNIA AS A FIELD FOR EMIGRATION,	80
VIII. "OUT AND ABOUT,"	89
IX. SEASIDE ON THE PACIFIC,	97
X. SAN FRANCISCO,	105
XI. NORTHWARDS TO BRITISH COLUMBIA,	115
XII. THE GREAT CANADIAN HIGHLANDS,	126
XIII. THE NORTH-WEST, MANITOBA, AND TORONTO,	130
XIV. NIAGARA,	138
XV. NORTHFIELD AND HOME,	144
APPENDIX—PROHIBITION IN THE UNITED STATES,	149

SUMMER SUNS IN THE FAR WEST.

CHAPTER I.

EDINBURGH TO PHILADELPHIA.

IT was on a chequered day of April 1889 that, leaving home for a long furlough, my wife and I got on board the *Furnessia* at Greenock, amid the usual excitement over luggage, and the terror lest some package intended for present use should lose its way and wander into the hold. An Edinburgh winter is a somewhat serious thing both for men and women who are not altogether backward in the service of the public, and a long holiday seemed very desirable for both, if we were to return to harness, and spend the evening of life in active service. Having a married son near Los Angeles, in Southern California, we determined to direct our footsteps thither and spend a few weeks in that semi-fabulous region. Some of our worthy friends thought that, being well on in the sixties, we were fit for the lunatic asylum in undertaking such a journey at our time of life. We pointed out that modern travel had been reduced to the simplest of arts: that we had just to go on board the steamer at Greenock and come out of it at New York; that if we pleased we might then go on board a Pullman car at New York, loll in an easy-chair by day and repose in a sleeping-berth by night, and come out six days after at Los Angeles; and that the risks incurred were really not much greater than in the Morningside street car, or the ferry-boat to Burntisland. Still, wise people shook their heads. And very emphatically the directors of an insurance company shook their corporate head, when I wished to purchase from them a couple of accident policies. After extra premiums had been clapped on for travelling in America, and other adjustments made, the arrangement suddenly collapsed at the eleventh hour. It turned out that at our age accident policies would not be granted on any terms! No wise company would vouch for such decrepit lives. I confess I was more amused than disappointed at the extraordinary caution of the worthy directors, though there was no time to apply elsewhere. We were led to think more of the unseen Protector. Anyhow, we did not mind the refusal; possibly because grapes have a way of turning sour when you cannot reach them.

Happily our luggage came together all right, and our berths were fairly comfortable; but it was midnight before we weighed anchor, and the working of the engine and rattling of the chains, as the crew kept lowering the cargo, gave us a concert of the most hideous music under which weary pilgrims ever tried to woo sleep. Morning, as usual, found us at Moville, on the north coast of Ireland, where we took on board our Celtic contingent in wonderfully good condition. Twice before I had witnessed the same process at Queenstown; but whether it was that Moville is in Ulster, or that the condition of the Irish peasantry has improved, our present emigrant cargo was by far the best-conditioned I had ever seen. I remember noticing once at Queenstown that though numberless girls were almost in rags, there was none that wanted a gum-flower; and the toilet of one poor girl attracted my special notice, she having a boot on one foot and a shoe on the other. There was nothing of this sort on board the *Furnessia*. All told, we were more than twelve hundred souls on board, and on the whole we were a happy family. The weather was cold but not rough, and there was a minimum amount of sea-sickness. We got very friendly with one another: it is wonderful how friendly you become during a voyage; and, alas! it is wonderful how soon your friendships pass out of mind.

There is not much variety of scenery on the Atlantic. Our one excitement was a shoal of big whales, some of which came so near the ship that we were almost able to make their individual acquaintance. Sunday brings a change— a pleasant change, I cannot help thinking, to most. I conducted service on both Sundays, both in the saloon and on the foredeck. Good Friday seemed likely to pass without any recognition, till a deputation from the intermediate cabin came to me and asked me to hold service there. It was an awkward place, but the service was the heartiest of any we held. There can be little privacy for intermediate and steerage passengers; and each evening the intermediates had a concert, or recitations, or something of that sort, in their diningroom to keep them lively. On Good Friday they thought they ought to be more serious—*paulo majora canamus*. It is easy to touch the feelings of emigrants, with their native shores behind them and an unknown future before them. To them it is no mere figure of speech when life is called a pilgrimage. Never is "O God of Bethel" more appropriate, never is a brighter welcome given to those truths which look forward to the end of the pilgrimage, and the gathering together in the Father's house.

It was on a Sunday night that we sighted the lights about Sandy Hook, and soon after greeted the electric blaze from the great Statue of Liberty. Monday morning we were astir by five o'clock, and an hour or two later were safely moored at the Anchor Wharf. As this was my third visit, I had no new sensations, but could enjoy the interest of fresher passengers looking out for the first time on the American shore. But I well remembered the sensation of my own first visit, at the marvellous metamorphosis which the shore presented as compared with former times: instead of the Red Indian with his plume waving over his head and his tomahawk by his side, one looked out on magnificent cities, whose wharves and docks, railways and steamboats, churches and colleges, and smiling suburban villas, proclaimed the triumph of industry and art. There used to be a story of a Pope asking an American pilgrim to the Vatican whether the aborigines or the English were the more numerous in New York! But we must pass in haste from the sentimental to the battle of life, and submit the contents of our travelling-boxes to the keen eye of the custom-house officer. Whether he was overawed by our respectability, or otherwise impressed in our favour, we know not, but he gave us a very easy inspection. We bade a hasty adieu to our fellow-passengers—such of them as were within reach—and in half-an-hour were comfortably quartered in the Grand Union Hotel.

My long and well-known connection with the General Presbyterian Alliance (called by the public the "Pan-Presbyterian," and by the profane the "Pan"), which brings Americans and Scotsmen into right friendly relations, procured for me an unexpected welcome. Before I had left the steamer, a minute of the American branch was placed in my hands, couched in very complimentary terms, welcoming me to America, and appointing my dear friend Dr. Schaff and three other friends to look after me in New York, and hold some kind of public meeting. The public meeting was out of the question, for I was unable to remain long enough in

New York; but Dr. Schaff was kind enough to invite some friends to his house, and we had a most pleasant evening. In a New York paper, *The Scottish American*, the company was given, all well-known in New York—Dr. and Mrs. Talbot Chambers, Dr. and Mrs. John Hall, Dr. and Mrs. Cuyler, Dr. and Mrs. Waters, Dr. and Mrs. J. S. Hamilton, Dr. and Mrs. Ellinwood, Professors Shedd, Briggs, Hastings, Brown, and Vincent; S. B. Brownell, Esq., Dr. Field, and many others. I could only utter my hearty thanks for so kind a welcome, all the more that I was travelling in an entirely private capacity, and the last thing I was looking for was such a recognition. It was a good opportunity for expressing what has long been one of my very earnest feelings—the desire that nothing may ever happen to disturb the friendly relations of the two great branches of the English people, as Professor Freeman has called them, but that Britain and the United States may ever move on hand in hand, united and cordial, in every measure fitted to advance the civilization and the Christianization of the world.

New York was all astir with preparations for the celebration of the Washington Centennial, which came off about this time. But it would detain me too long to describe that or any other New York scene. I was greatly interested in the sermon of Bishop Potter, in which he made a bold and earnest effort to restore the political life of the country to the state of purity it enjoyed when it bore the impress of Washington's noble character. It was amusing to watch the newspaper war which followed. It was too strong a dose for those patriots who can stomach nothing but eulogy and admiration; but it struck a deep chord in all the nobler souls of the country. The universal and simultaneous honour paid to the memory of Washington by so many millions of people could hardly fail of good result. It could not but be useful to remember that the one thing that made him great was his honest and profound regard for the welfare of his people, and that what endeared his memory to millions, and made them proud of him, was his patient devotion to duty, his sacrifice of self, his indifference to wealth, honour, and pleasure—his one object in life to serve his country. "Go, and do thou likewise," seemed the appropriate application to every public man in America of every oration, sermon, or speech delivered on the occasion.

Among the objects which I was anxious to accomplish during this visit, one was to get at the truth respecting the prohibition movement in the country. One hears such opposite opinions. "A great success and blessing," say some; "an utter failure," say others. "As much drink consumed under nominal prohibition as before, with the addition that the law is brought into contempt, and with the further addition that the drink is dearer in price and worse in quality." "A wonderful increase of both material and moral prosperity." The truth, I knew, must lie between these extremes, but whereabout between?

Within the last few days the state of Massachusetts had voted decidedly against prohibition, as the state of Pennsylvania did afterwards, when the question was tried there in June. I called on Mr. Maynard of the *New York Observer*, who had been quite recently appointed a commissioner by that paper to travel about and make full inquiry on the subject. Mr. Maynard had just returned from a three weeks' tour in the state of Kansas, in which he had made inquiry of all sorts of people—friends and foes, judges and magistrates, jailers and policemen, ministers and merchants—on the results of prohibition. His report was eminently favourable. Not only was prohibition the law, but it was strictly enforced there, and even rich men who had violated it were sent remorselessly to prison. Crime and disorder of every kind had marvellously decreased. Mr. Maynard had begun a series of articles in the *New York Observer* giving the results of his inquiry. I asked him what he thought of the Massachusetts vote. He said he was not in the least surprised. Prohibition was a very strong measure, and like the abolition of slavery, it would cost many a battle to achieve it. He had the firmest confidence that in the course of time it would prevail universally in America, and would be as decidedly held to be the right thing as the abolition of slavery was now. I asked him about the high-license system which now exists in some states. Licenses in some instances cannot be got under £200. Mr. Maynard did not think they had done any such good as to render the agitation for prohibition superfluous. Other friends whom I have consulted are more friendly to the high-license system. It has shut up an immense number of low drinking-saloons, but of course it has brought increased custom to the richer drink-sellers. One thing I see very clearly: one must make careful discrimination between one place and another in deciding what measures are best for temperance reform.

Short though our time was in New York, we resolved to have a glance at two things—the Central Park and the Brooklyn Bridge. Nineteen years ago I had visited the Park, which was then only beginning to awake to a consciousness of what it might become. I well remember the quarry holes, the heaps of rubbish, and profusion of ungainly things scattered abroad. But this wilderness has blossomed as the rose. In a friend's carriage we drove luxuriously over the gravel paths, through groves of greenery tastefully brightened by the blaze of flowers and the gleam of marble statuary. The carriage drives were dotted with mounted police, trained to catch runaway horses whether attached to carriages or loose. The gallery of art and the museum of natural history have been placed in the Park, as well as the zoological collection, as inducements to the citizens to make it a place of frequent resort. Perhaps some of our corporations at home might take a hint from this. As for Brooklyn Bridge, it is a marvellous structure to be hung on a couple of chains. Nine years ago, if I remember rightly, a slim line like a spider's thread was all that was visible—a small beginning for so wonderful a result. I found it difficult to convince Americans that our Forth Bridge was a vaster undertaking, and that they would need to apply themselves to something still greater if they aspired to own the most notable bridge in the world.

Though California was our destination, we had so many kind friends in some of the eastern states that we arranged to spend a few days at Philadelphia, Baltimore, Cincinnati, and Chicago on our westward way. And everywhere we were received with such hospitality that our great difficulty was to break away. We had to complain that, though going ahead was the great feature of the country, they would not let us go ahead.

Philadelphia had a special interest; for it was there the reunited General Assembly, to which I was sent as a delegate from the Free Church, was held in 1870; and it was there, too, that the second General Presbyterian Council (the "Pan") met in 1880. Alas! not a few of our dearest friends both in Philadelphia and New York had passed away in the interval. It was pleasant to see that, as the old standard-bearers fell, there were other men to take the colours. The Women's Foreign Missionary Society, a great institution, which has flourished wonderfully, and greatly promoted the mission cause, was holding its annual meeting, attended by more than five hundred women. My wife was carried off to the meeting, and received a most gratifying reception. She was much struck by the business capacity and great energy of the American women. During the year they have collected 145,000 dollars—say nearly £30,000.

They have one hundred and forty-six missionaries in foreign countries, of whom seventy have been sent out during the year. It would be worth while to give a full statement of their work, as contained in their annual report, and, what would be even more interesting, a statement of their methods. But space forbids further reference. One of the secretaries of the society was the daughter of our host.

A son in the same family was secretary to the Christian Endeavour Society. This is a society having objects somewhat similar to that of our guilds at home. But while the society is so far denominational that each congregation has its own branch, the whole is united in one great confederation, somewhat like the Presbyterian Alliance. The society holds a great annual meeting, which took place this year at Philadelphia. My friend was busy with preparations. It was expected that four thousand at least would be present—not all as delegates. I think the actual number was between six and seven thousand. There were members present from California and other far-distant parts of the country. Distance is no bugbear to American travellers.

Philadelphia is building a magnificent city hall, on a magnificent site at the union of Broad and High Streets. The only pity is that the building obstructs the continuous view which there used to be from end to end of these fine streets. The new erection is of marble; and as it has to wait for annual appropriations of money from the city, it advances but slowly towards completion. A new feature of Philadelphia, as also of New York, is the immense blocks of offices and other business chambers, for which eight stories is now a moderate height. The enormous cost of building areas necessitates this arrangement. The old Edinburgh houses of ten or twelve stories are being left behind. I heard an American repeat the somewhat apocryphal story of a man who, in falling from the top of one of the tall Edinburgh houses, passed a servant girl cleaning a window about the fifth story, and remarked to her, "Eh, lassie, sic a *clype* I'm gaein' to get;" but it might be fathered now on New York or Philadelphia. There is no trouble getting to the top of these Titanic houses, for they are all furnished with one or more "elevators," or, as we should call them, "lifts," which land you in a few seconds in any story you wish to visit. Hydraulic pressure furnishes the power, and the only drawback to your satisfaction is pity for the monotonous life of the man or boy in charge, engaged all day long in working the apparatus.

The Americans have a wonderful way of scenting out men (and women too) who are supposed to be able to speak in public. Professor Shaw of Lincoln University, son-in-law of an old friend (his wife is a daughter of the late Rev. William Arnot of Edinburgh), found us out at Philadelphia, and invited us to pay a visit to his college. Mr. Shaw being an old student of mine at Edinburgh, and his wife an old friend of us both, brief though our time was, we could not but accept the invitation. Lincoln University is situated between Philadelphia and Baltimore, and is designed for training men of colour for the ministry. It is of recent origin; and though it has made excellent progress during its short career, the term "university" (as in many other instances in America) denotes not what it already is, but what it aspires to be. Though under Presbyterian auspices, it is open to young men of all evangelical denominations; and it has no fewer than one hundred and sixty students. The only department of the university thoroughly equipped is the theological. Professor Shaw has the chair of Hebrew, and he maintains stoutly that negro students are as capable as any other of proficiency in Hebrew, and indeed in all other branches of liberal study. He maintains that the mixture of blood is not the explanation of this, inasmuch as students of pure blood are just as capable as those of mixed. This, I know, is not the universal opinion; for instance, Mr. Moody, who has a great power of knowing men, does not regard the negro as equal in capacity to other races.

Of course there was a reception, and I was introduced to the professors and their wives, and to some of the ministers and residents in the surrounding district. One gentleman introduced himself to me as the first professor of the English Bible in any college in the world. He drills the students in the Bible, making them commit to memory many suitable passages, and sustain examinations on important portions of it. Men of colour are not the only students who would be better for this exercise.

Before I got to Lincoln, Professor Shaw had wired me for a "talk." I agreed to give a lecture on Livingstone and Africa, though I had no written materials, and happily it interested them quite remarkably. Some of them were preparing for service in Africa, and the name of Livingstone was dear to them all. In fact, the hall in which I lectured was called Livingstone Hall, having been the gift of an admirer of the great missionary. A black student opened with an excellent prayer, and another closed. In a Presbyterian divinity college there is little scope for negro eccentricity, such as we often hear of. The men work for their maintenance during the recess, and for the most part pay the cost of board. They are not at all particular as to what they work at. At Professor Shaw's we were served by a coloured waiter in full black dress and copious linen breast. He was one of the students, or "boys," as the professor called them, and his business was that of a waiter. In towns like Baltimore it is said that some negroes have made a little fortune by "waiting."

There are two points connected with the negro race on which I was desirous to get information—negro religion and negro social prospects. It is well known that the great majority of the negroes, especially down south, are either Baptists or Methodists. Under the shadow of these systems they have more scope to indulge their native tastes. The element that predominates in their religion is the emotional. They are fond of singing hymns, of appeals to the senses and the imagination, but do not usually care for appeals to the intellect and the conscience. I was told, for instance, of a native preacher who had given out one of the commandments for his text, when a hearer rose up and told him, "We don't want to hear nothing of that sort here; you stop, and give us the gospel." It reminded me of what I had heard of a negro woman who had stolen a goose but would not own it, that one Sabbath morning she informed her mistress that she was going to the communion. Her mistress remonstrated, as she had never "'fessed the goose." "Well, madam," she said, "I don't deny that I did take it; but if you suppose that for the matter of one goose I am going to deny my Saviour, you are much mistaken." On a certain plantation there was a most eloquent and powerful negro preacher. There had been much depredation on the plantation, and it occurred to the owner to enlist the services of the preacher to deliver a sermon against stealing. He said he understood he was a very impressive preacher. The negro in reply "guessed he could do it pretty smart." He then asked him to preach a sermon on honesty. The preacher's face assumed a strange look. No, he said, he could not do that; for if he gave out such a subject, it would throw quite a chill over the congregation. On the other hand, I have heard of negroes and negro preachers as blameless and pure of life as the whitest of the white. And some of them are powerful preachers, despite their grotesque composition and pronunciation. At Lincoln University, and I have no doubt at other seminaries, the tone of instruction gives an emphatic check to any divorce of religion and morality.

With regard to negro social prospects, the problem of the future is just where it was. No appreciable progress has been made in the way of amalgamating the two races with each other. The churches are feeling themselves obliged to agree to some compromise on the subject. The difficulty of bringing black and white into one baffles all of them. Coloured people don't commonly like white ministers, and white people have still more determined objections to black pastors. When a Synod or an Assembly meets at any place, no white family will take in a coloured delegate. The consequence is that virtually separate churches have to be formed for white and black. The Methodist Church has a coloured Conference, and the Southern Presbyterian Church has a coloured Synod. In some sense these are parts of the white organization, but otherwise they are separate. When I was in Baltimore I found that two of my friends in that city—Dr. Joseph Smith, and Dr. Leftwich, of the First Presbyterian Church, for both of whom I officiated—had just been south, conferring with delegates from the Southern Church on co-operation in work among the negroes, and it was in this direction that their proposals ran. It is disappointing to find that we are so far from a satisfactory solution of the problem; but it is a characteristic of the American people not to wait till they can secure the optimist arrangement of any question, but to do the best they can in the circumstances. If America had not made good use of this rule, it would never have been the country that it is.

CHAPTER II.

BALTIMORE TO CHICAGO.

OUR next visit was to Baltimore. It is a fine city, with more of the air of Old England about it than most cities in the States. It derives its name from an English nobleman, and traditions of the olden time seem to hover over it, as if loath to depart. We had a particularly warm reception from the friends who entertained us in Baltimore. They represented a family of some mark that had been long settled in the city. We had made their acquaintance in Switzerland some years before. We could not but recall the family of Philip the evangelist, but instead of four daughters who were virgins our host had seven, and instead of prophesying they were all busily engaged in Christian labours of love.

The city has a wonderfully fine park—Druid Hill. It was in great beauty, greatly improved since our first visit. I believe it was formerly the property of some scrubby old man that would let nobody into it; now it belongs to the citizens, and they do enjoy it, from the least even to the greatest. A well-frequented park has a great social effect, drawing a community together, and forming a bond between rich and poor. And the gold of the evening sun, stealing through leafy thickets, and transfiguring all with heavenly glory, has a thrilling effect, one would hope a good effect, sluggish though human beings are to respond to the silent influences of nature.

The sensation of Baltimore was over the approaching opening of the Johns-Hopkins Hospital. It must be explained that Mr. Johns-Hopkins was a very rich merchant, far from open-handed in his lifetime, who, when he could keep his seven millions of dollars no longer, left them to found two institutions—a university and a hospital. Through the kindness of President Gillman we were shown over the university buildings ; and another officer showed us the hospital, which was opened publicly the day after we left. Both are on a very high scale, especially the hospital. Every contrivance for the benefit of the sick and for the efficient carrying on of the work of the hospital that modern skill has discovered is brought into full play in the arrangements. I believe the architect was sent over the world to inspect all the chief hospitals in existence, and get from them every arrangement that experience had devised for their efficient management. The university has been chiefly distinguished for physical research. Its many publications have already procured for it a distinguished place, and it seems likely that it will accomplish much more. I found considerable anxiety prevailing in Christian families on account of the appointment of some professors whose views inclined to scepticism. Christian parents did not like to place their sons under the shadow of unbelievers, whatever might be the branch of study, and some young men had gone to Princeton who would naturally have studied at the Johns-Hopkins. It is believed, however, that the trustees will be more careful in future appointments. The college is undenominational, and, like other American colleges, is governed by a body of trustees, the first having been named by the testator. The hospital is a fine and imposing building; but the university is scattered over a considerable number of separate erections, and none of them is sufficiently imposing to correspond to the importance of the institution.

Some of the marble houses of Baltimore are very beautiful. But there is a green-stone in the neighbourhood with which architects are but too prone to play fantastic tricks. A church which presents sundry stripes of this green-stone has gained from an irreverent public the name of "The Church of the Holy Zebra." It brought to mind a church in another city, with a tall and very narrow spire, which has suggested the name of "The Church of the Sacred Toothpick." We cannot linger over the institutions of Baltimore, but the Peabody Institute, with its large library and art collection, deserves special notice—a link of connection between the old country and the new, and a token of that cordial feeling which made Mr. Peabody the benefactor of both.

Our friends at Baltimore had arranged for us a day's pleasant excursion to Washington. We were greatly struck with the improvement of the capital during the last nineteen years. Thackeray's designation "the city of magnificent distances" is applicable no longer. Its vacant stances are now occupied by handsome public buildings and private residences. The trees lining the residential streets, that were mere saplings in our recollection, are now of tolerable size. The carriage-ways, that used to be so rugged, are paved with asphalt. For once in an American city you see not a few symbols of royalty, but it is over the doors of the foreign embassies. Great Britain of course mounts the lion and the unicorn over her embassy—a respectable residence with very little style. The most remarkable change in Washington is the completion of the National Monument. It is a plain obelisk, towering to the height of above five hundred feet, traversed in the interior by an elevator, which, if you can secure a place in it, will carry you to the top in less than ten minutes. There you will find a magnificent view of the meandering Potomac at your feet, and of the other objects of interest about Washington, round and round. If you descend by the stair, you will find an opportunity of reading the names of the states, cities, companies, Sabbath schools, societies, and individuals that contributed to the building of the monument. I could not but think of the great Christian temple of the apostle, that glorious edifice to the erection of which all tribes and peoples and tongues are to contribute their share.

We had hoped to have a private interview with the President, but by some unexpected *contretemps* we did not succeed. So we went with all the world to the White House at one o'clock, merely to shake hands. As soon as the clock struck, the worthy gentleman came into the room by a door in the farther end, as quietly as possible, and stood rather helplessly near it, as the citizens crowded past. He looked substantial, but by no means brilliant. There was no little business power evinced in his face, such as you might expect in a successful Indianapolis lawyer, who had the reputation of having seldom or never lost a case. He is an elder of the Presbyterian Church, and at Indianapolis was actively interested in church work. His father-in-law, the Rev. Dr. Scott, a very aged man, resides with the family. Mr. Harrison has laid down a rule for himself that he will do no business on Sunday. He claims it as the day of rest, and maintains that the President needs rest as much as the poorest mechanic. Another step in the direction of Sabbath rest has been taken by Mr. Wanamaker, the postmaster-general. The doors of the Washington office are closed every Sunday. I am happy to say that there seems to be a general movement in the country at present in favour of a better observance of the Lord's day. Many of the railway companies are reducing the number of freight trains and excursion trains. The want of a Sabbath in many parts of the country is recognized by them as hurtful to the physical welfare of the people, as it is by others to their moral and spiritual good.

The civil service of the United States has got into such a bad groove that it must be extremely difficult for any President to move it into a better. Innumerable situations throughout the whole country are thrown vacant at every presidential election, and it has been too much the practice of the new President to reward his friends by the gift of these. As far as I could learn, the new President is honestly trying to continue efficient men of whatever party in office, and remove those only whose qualifications are deficient, or who were placed in office for mere political ends. But the matter is often complicated, and probably he will not fully please either party.

Dr. Hamlin, minister of a very handsome Presbyterian church, called the Church of the Covenant, had asked me to take part in his service next day, but previous engagements prevented. The President holds a pew there, Mr. Secretary Blaine another, Secretary of Treasury Windom a third, and Postmaster Wanamaker a fourth. It might almost be called the Church of the Cabinet. It is a recent erection, and cost upwards of 200,000 dollars. One day the spire subsided; it did not even fall over on the road, but simply sat down, having been badly built. A good many thousand dollars were needed to build it up. It is one proof of the greater wealth of America that sums are often expended on church building that would simply overwhelm us in Scotland. It must be remembered that a complete church establishment embraces not only the church proper, but a chapel for lesser gatherings, Sabbath-school buildings to any amount, parlours for committee and other meetings, a pastor's study and a pastor's house, all fitted up with handsome carpets and other furniture, the cost of the whole probably double that of a church alone. Christian liberality is a marvel to the world, even though it has far from reached the limit of its capacity.

From Baltimore our destination was Cincinnati, distant

six hundred miles. We had to find our way through the Alleghany Mountains, and far from an easy way it was for the railway. But the route from Harrisburg to Pittsburg, which occupies the greater part of the day, is extremely beautiful. Along sweet river-sides and through wooded mountains, by banks and braes that are well deserving of a poet's song, you are whirled along in a constant succession of beauty. At the famous "horse-shoe" the line has to double upon itself—an operation of which we afterwards came on some much more extensive specimens. Among the towns we passed was ill-fated Johnstown, reposing softly in the mellow sunshine, with its busy population of 30,000. Had we only known what was to happen, we should not have been satisfied with the cursory, careless look that hardly impressed its features on our memory. It was but a week or two after that a dam burst a few miles higher up the valley, creating a tragedy of destruction hardly paralleled in history, the loss of life being variously stated between fifteen thousand and three thousand. At the time of the accident we were near Los Angeles, and from one of its ministers, the Rev. J. L. Russell, who had quite recently been transferred from Altona, in the immediate neighbourhood of Johnstown, and who was intimately acquainted with many of the sufferers, we learned some sad particulars that had not appeared in the newspapers. Among these was the case of a young lady who had been borne away on a piece of wreck, and remained in the water sixteen hours, terribly buffeted. Her clothes were torn off her, and she was utterly exhausted when she was found by her brother. He had to clothe her with some of his own garments, and carry her on his back six miles before he could get anything done for her. Some people were reported dead, or at least mad, who were really safe. Among these was a Mr. Fulton, a gentleman in good business, and president of the

Amendment Committee—that is, the committee that was then trying to get prohibition carried in Pennsylvania. A friend meeting him congratulated him on being alive, and alluded to the rumour that he was dead. "Did you not know," said he, "that I could not die before the 18th of June?" That was to be the great voting day. The newspapers were full of tales, all tales of tragedy, but many of heroism and noble effort. Conspicuous among these was the case of an unknown horseman, who, when he saw the water beginning to rush out at the bottom of the embankment, galloped down the valley, exhorting all to escape to the mountains, but was himself swept away and swallowed up in the roaring flood.

We reached Cincinnati after a night in the sleeping cars. Under the kind charge of Dr. Morris of Lane Theological Seminary, we had a most agreeable visit here—"a good time," though hurried—were introduced to many of the citizens, and feasted by a brother Scot who rejoices in the title of the "oil-king." Cincinnati is a prosperous and remarkable city, was once the rival of Chicago, but has been outstripped in the race by its old competitor. I cannot but note a little fact that gave me no ordinary satisfaction. A poor boy, who had been a scholar in the Sunday school at Pilrig when I was minister there, had found his way to Cincinnati, and having procured for himself a training as a lawyer, was now one of the foremost lawyers, and one of the most exemplary and liberal Christians, of the city. Well do I remember the dingy house in which his family lived, in that same dingy street, then called Moray Street (Spey Street now), where Thomas Carlyle spent some years of his Edinburgh life; and well do I remember the feelings with which I used to call on that boy's mother, and another worthy mother in the same stair, both struggling hard to bring up large families aright, amid great difficulty and much sorrow. They did need comfort, for they were fighting a hard but noble battle; and both of them had great cause to thank God for his blessing, which in the evening of their life came in more forms than one. Bread cast on the water *is* found after many days. Apart from the personal aspect of the case, I looked on it as a remarkable illustration of the openness of the path to success and distinction in the United States. The poorest boy (James Garfield, for instance) may find his way to the very top of the ladder. Cincinnati brought me another joy. An esteemed minister told me he knew of two, if not three, young men who had been led to devote themselves to foreign missions through reading the "Personal Life of Livingstone."

From Cincinnati a day's travelling brought us to Chicago. Chicago is everywhere a household word, the symbol of marvellous progress and extraordinary enterprise. But every one knows about Chicago. Two pleasant visits were paid to the Presbyterian and Congregational theological seminaries, in the latter of which I found an old student of New College, Edinburgh—Professor Scott—enjoying a high reputation both as a professor and a preacher. The Presbyterian seminary owes not a little to the late Mr. M'Cormick, after whom it is named, well known among our farmers in connection with the M'Cormick reaping-machine; and it is a pleasure to add that his son is following in his steps. Part of our little time at Chicago was spent under the roof of the widow of one of the earliest traders in the place—the late Mr. Hubbard, who settled at Fort Dearborn when there were but two houses in the neighbourhood. He became a very prosperous citizen, and owned a fine house and garden in the city. When the great fire broke out on the other side of the river, there was no idea that it would cross over to his neighbourhood. After it had burned for many hours, his wife at night was looking sadly out at the blazing city, and seeing an unusual brightness, begged Mr. Hubbard (who was in bed) to come and look at it. Seeing the direction the fire was taking, he became alarmed, roused his household, filled his carriages with books, pictures, and whatever else of value was portable, and sent the whole to the houses of friends at a distance. Ere long the house was burned to the ground. Some of his furniture was stolen, but was afterwards discovered in a house in the suburbs, and recovered by its rightful owner. Mr. Hubbard never rebuilt his house, and the site on which it stood, with a cavity in the centre, stands to this day, a touching memorial of one of the greatest calamities that have happened in modern times. How many stories of the like kind might Chicago tell!

The chief interest of my visit to Chicago was in connection with Mr. Moody. He was just at the end of a month's labour in his own church, which is situated in the north end of the town, in the immediate neighbourhood of Mrs. Hubbard's house, not far from the site of Dearborn Fort. The spot where he commenced his home mission work when an employé in a shoe-store is not far off. It was a great pleasure to meet again the prince of evangelists, and find him directing all his energies to make his work more aggressive, and to train agents to go to the haunts of sinners and urge the careless to come in. It seemed to me that unconsciously, perhaps, he was taking a lesson from Dr. Chalmers. He was very particular in urging that, when the careless did come in, they should get a repast suited to their wants, and not be chilled by that cold formality which seemed to him the bane of all the churches. I was twice in his church, on a week-day and on the Sabbath. Both times he constrained me to give a word. I heard him give a lecture on the thirteenth chapter of 1st Corinthians, and afterwards at

Northfield I heard him preach on subjects equally practical. I asked him whether he was not preaching more than he used to do on the application of Christianity to daily life. "Yes, I am," he replied. The readiness of human nature to abuse free grace had impressed itself on him, and the need of "line upon line, precept upon precept," had become a burning conviction. But Moody knew well what many do not know—how to connect the inculcation of a thorough obedience in every-day life with living faith in Christ, and not doom poor weak human nature to struggles and burdens for which its strength is quite unequal.

I was more than ever impressed with the fact that Moody is a man *sui generis*. There will never be a school of Moodys. His methods will not be carried out in full by other men. But besides the success of his evangelistic work, he will always be remarkable for the impulse which he imparts to Christian workers towards plainness of speech, earnestness, and consecration. There will likewise be a constant increase of reverence for the Bible under his instructions and example. Moody is a man of one book, and it is a singular testimony to the everlasting freshness and fulness of the Bible that everything which he ever has taught, or ever will teach, is derived from it alone. I rather think that now that he is entering on the work of permanent organization he will find that what to him has been a strong point hitherto is really a weak point—I mean his being unconnected officially with any branch of the Church, and his acting solely on his own responsibility.

We had no time to see much more of Chicago on this occasion than a saunter through the streets and a drive through its fine Lincoln Park and other suburbs allowed. One institution, however, did command our special attention —the Women's Christian Temperance Union. It is always known as the W.C.T.U., letters of which the saloon-keepers have their own interpretation—"Women constantly torment us." Its office is in one of the largest blocks in one of the chief commercial streets. The building—it all belongs to the W.C.T.U.—cost 800,000 dollars, but a great part of it is let out for offices and warerooms, the rent going to pay interest on mortgages. But the temperance women have very large accommodation for themselves. They have business offices, and editorial sanctums, and an entire printing and publishing establishment. The lady secretaries and the lady editor seem quite at home in their places of business and in the whole round of their work. The weekly temperance journal, the *Union Signal*, with a circulation of above fifty thousand copies, is edited and published by them. The president of the Union is Miss Willard, usually regarded as the most eloquent woman in America. Miss Willard is one of those who have strongly urged the formation of "a third party,"—that is, a party whose one object shall be to secure prohibition, and which will support any prohibitionist candidate, be he republican or democratic. This action, however, does not meet with the approval of all the temperance party (and I agree with them), both because they dislike mixing up their cause with party politics, and because they do not consider the policy in itself to be the best for the temperance cause. But the women's establishment looks like business, and shrewd vigorous women they seemed who were at work within its walls.

CHAPTER III.

PRAIRIE AND COLORADO ROCKIES.

WE took our tickets by the Chicago and Union Pacific line right from Chicago to our final destination, Los Angeles, with "stop-over" rights by the way; and I have to acknowledge the courtesy of the railway authorities, both of this and other American lines, in allowing me to travel at the rates which clergymen of the country are usually charged. We left Chicago about mid-day, and nothing could have been more delightful than the motion of the Pullman car in which we had our seats. Whether it had more india-rubber in its construction than other cars, or whether the level surface of the prairie made it run more smoothly, certain it is that its motion was hardly more perceptible than that of the earth itself. We moved all afternoon and evening through the pleasant prairie country, admiring the level fields, and the soil as rich and soft and loose as if it were all mole-heaps, looking as if the plough might glide through it as easily as a boat through water. It was easy now to understand how these prairies were so admirably adapted for raising grain and cattle. About seven in the evening we came on the Mississippi. It was our first sight of the king of waters. I am afraid I am of very gross temperament, for the sight impressed me but little. There was of course a large body of water, but what one missed was some visible mark of imperial grandeur. There were no high banks like those of the Rhine, no impetuous defiant rush like the rapids of Niagara, no visible memorials of majesty and power. You need to draw on your logical faculty, your multiplication table, and your imagination to realize the vastness of the Mississippi, and its claim as king of waters. But it is truly a grand river, and a man feels himself bigger after he has seen it.

Most of the state of Iowa we traversed during the night. It is inevitable in American travelling that you lose a good deal by travelling in the dark. There is some fine scenery, I believe, near Des Moines, the capital of Iowa, but most of the road is over prairie. In the morning we were approaching another great river, the Missouri. The "bluffs" in the Missouri valley are conspicuous and attractive. "Council Bluffs" is the name of a thriving little city. On the other side of the Missouri is the quite recent and very flourishing city of Omaha, the capital of another state, Nebraska, which is separated from Iowa by the river.

Not very many years ago, "west of the Missouri" meant something like "the back o' beyont," in old country phrase. It is here that "new America" begins. Professor Freeman might have added another England to his list, and found four Englands instead of three. I used often when in America to repeat his remark that the English were all one people; that wherever they lived was England; that the first England was the little territory between Denmark and Prussia whence the Angli sprang; the second England the island in the German Ocean where the first set of emigrants settled; and the third, commonly called New England, the shores of the continent where another body of emigrants of the same stock made their home. What I claim as the fourth England is the region west of the Missouri, peopled substantially by the same race. And without prejudice to the merits of all the earlier Englands, these "new Englanders," as they may emphatically be called, who have made their home in this far west, have got a country that for gifts of nature may hold its head as high, if not higher, than any of them.

We knew that a group of half-German half-Scotch cousins, who were settled some forty miles from Omaha, would give us a very cordial welcome, and we resolved to spend a day with them. Before our train started, we had time to take "a hack" and drive through Omaha and its suburbs. I need not say it was a place undreamt of when I learned my geography. But in truth what could geography say, in my day, of that chain of remarkable cities—Chicago, Omaha, Denver, and Salt Lake City—that are the great landmarks between New York and San Francisco? What could it say of San Francisco itself? Omaha has been made by the Pacific Railway Company. The bluffs about it afford ample variety of ground, and form fine sites for public buildings and private villas. I do not know whether the massive mercantile blocks in the centre of such towns or the beautiful villas in the suburbs give one the more vivid idea of prosperity. It struck me, not with reference to Omaha merely, but the suburbs of other cities, that American architects must have been giving great attention of late to villa architecture. Many a chaste and beautiful design we saw from first to last; but as all the villas, at least with very few exceptions, are of wood, the architect has a more pliable material to deal with than in the old country, and yet I should think that he is far from having exhausted the forms of which villa architecture is susceptible in wood.

Our cousins were settled some five miles from a station called Newaka, on a new line of railway. Meeting us was the inevitable "buggy," and we drove pleasantly over primitive roads, very agreeable when not too dusty, utterly innocent of macadamizing or any such barbarous process; first because there were no stones to macadamize with, and second, because the traffic was not great enough to require it. The group of cousins embraced three families, two of them farmers, the third, who prided himself on bearing the very name of the Irish Secretary, Arthur James Balfour, was postmaster. All of them were living simple, primitive, unconventional lives, the farmers their own landlords and their own tenants and servants too; for unless a man have a larger farm than the ordinary, he has to do his own work outside, while the womankind in like manner have to do all within. Whether the outcome of this mode of living shall be comfortable or comfortless, is by no means certain, but, as we say, *depends*. Diligence thrives, idleness wastes. One of the houses was a model of good order and comfort. The owner, still a youngish man, emigrated in childhood with his family from Germany; and his father having died from wounds received in the civil war, our friend began life on his own account with but a handful of dollars. But he was careful, steady, and laborious, and worked his way upwards till now he has a very desirable farm and a most comfortable establishment. This gentleman told us that to save house-building when he had no money to spare for it, he had lived at first in a sort of cave hollowed out from a steep hillside. After occupying this mansion for a while, a spring of water sprang up in the bottom of it, and however he might dodge it, or coax it to run off, or place big stones on the floor on which to step, the thing became too bad, and he had to abandon it for another dwelling. Prosperous men like our friend have a handy way of immortalizing themselves. Some publisher or speculator will get up a county history in a large quarto volume. Yes; even there, there are already county histories. A canvasser goes round the county, and to every man who subscribes five dollars promises a notice of his farm, while twenty or twenty-five dollars insures a place in the volume for the likeness of the subscriber. If you are not acquainted with this private arrangement, you will be at a loss to understand how these undistinguished prairies should possess so many distinguished men.

Next afternoon we return from Newaka to Omaha, and in the evening we are again in motion for Denver, the capital of Colorado. Again the night hides from us the prairies of Nebraska, as it had hid those of Iowa. The fine agricultural land of the east gives place after a time to the rich grazing country of the west, till next day we get among the "sand-hills" of Colorado, and have our first experience of the desert. It was a dreary day. Sometimes no more than a single shanty could be discerned all around. At other times, through some mysterious cause, probably the neighbourhood of a mine, we came on quite a little town. It was strange in such a situation to find a large wooden building surmounted in bold letters with the words "Theatre" or "Opera House," indicating the irrepressible love of amusement, made more intense no doubt by the monotony all around. More interesting to us was the belfry of the village school, or the spire of the village church. Very eloquent in such a place is the little home of the Christian Church. It attests the presence of men and women to whom getting rich is not the chief end of life, or who, at least, are conscious that it ought not so to be. We silently blessed the men who had planted it; and there arose a prayer from our hearts that these dwellers in the wilderness, who seemed to have so little to vary their earthly life, might enjoy much fellowship with Heaven, and find their souls refreshed, Sabbath by Sabbath, from the river that makes glad the city of our God.

But the longest lane has its turning. The Rocky Mountains heave in sight, and thrill you with a new sensation.

And at last you are in Denver, and find handsome and comfortable quarters in the Lincoln Hotel.

Denver is quite a remarkable city. Its prosperity is due mainly to the mineral treasures of Colorado; but its singularly exhilarating atmosphere and the glorious scenery of the Rocky Mountains all around have helped it on. It is finely situated on commanding plateaus; has wide streets and handsome blocks of warehouses and stores, and no end of pretty villas in the suburbs. We spent an afternoon riding through its streets and suburbs; but we were unfortunate in weather, for the evening was wet, and on the following morning there was snow. The wet weather brought out in perfection one of the outstanding features of Denver — its muddy streets. It was certainly a peculiar experience to find a city of some one hundred thousand inhabitants, with numberless tokens of prosperity and progress, in which the carriage-way of the streets was in a state of nature, and no lady could cross without having her boots encased in mud. We were glad to know that the Denver authorities had wakened up to this condition of things, and that steps were about to be taken for having the streets " fixed."

Denver was inundated that evening by a swarm of railway conductors, who were holding a convention and enjoying an excursion. "Conductors" are greater men than railway guards are with us. Mysterious badges worn by half the ladies and gentlemen in the Lincoln Hotel resolved themselves into symbols of this fraternity. We realized the significance of this convention the following night, for when we went to the Pullman office to secure sleeping-berths, we found to our disgust that all were taken. And when we got into the train next morning, we could hardly get places anywhere.

Denver is not only the capital of the great mining industries of Colorado, but also a centre of wonderfully fine

scenery. We had taken our tickets by the Rio Grande
route, because it passes over the sublimest scenery of the
Rocky Mountains; and during the whole of the day our
course lay through a constant succession of grandeur and
glory. Happily, at a junction not very far from Denver,
many of our fellow-passengers left us, so that we had room
enough during the remainder of our journey. Now we
would dash through canyons or gorges, wild as the Devil's
Bridge in Switzerland, formed by a narrow slit in the
mountain, with high perpendicular precipices on either
side; and now through passes beautiful as that of Kil-
liecrankie, but of a vastness and variety that dwarfed all
other scenery. The engine rushed wildly into the canyons,
dragging the train after it, even though it might seem that
our further progress was absolutely barred by the meeting
of the rocks; but it found a way of winding through, though
at times the road had to be supported on brackets fastened
to the rock, and at other times kept in position by stanchions
fixed overhead on the other wall of the chasm. So wonderful are the passes through which the line is carried that the
train obligingly stops at various points to give you a more
deliberate view; at one place you change into what is called
a "prospect" or open carriage, in order to have a better
view of the wonderful scenery. Further on in the day, the
train begins to climb the mountains until it reaches an
altitude of nearly ten thousand feet above the sea-level.
The gradients are so steep that it has to be divided in two,
and an extra engine attached to the bigger part of it. It is
Glen Ogle multiplied a hundredfold. Never does the iron
horse appear so noble an animal as when he dashes at the
mountain side, and tears along its precipices, dragging his
load after him as if it were but a feather; then turns and
doubles on himself, zig-zagging his course, till he has carried
you to the top of the first height, and looking down you see

the wonderful succession of terraces along which he has borne you. Without stopping to draw breath, he plunges, like Fitz-James's stag, into a bosky thicket, whirls you round a corner, and bravely sets himself to drag you up another reach of the mighty mountain, and so on until he has reached the top. Nightfall comes before the marvellous scenery is exhausted; but if you are favoured with moonlight you can see that your course is still through precipitous gorges and along banks of mountain streams, making you wish that, as in Joshua's days, the sun had only stood still for an hour or two to make their beauties more apparent.

At last you take to your night quarters. You look out in the morning—and where are you? In a very wilderness of sand! Nothing can exceed the desolation. And through this wilderness you are carried most of the day, but with new features of wonder breaking in upon you. For not only do you see against the sky a waving line of snow-clad summits, but nearer you the sandstone hills are rising in every variety of picturesque form, great ranges of Salisbury Crags, often with level battlements piled atop, and natural bits of crag that look like Tantallan Castles, or the ruined fortresses on "the castellated Rhine." Your engine needs to make another series of great efforts to pull you over the mountains; but at last, as evening again draws on, you are in the plain of Utah. That lake gleaming brightly on your left is Utah Lake—not the Salt Lake, however, which is considerably more to the north. You think of the poor Mormon pilgrims who had to do this journey on foot through weary weeks and months, amid heat and thirst and pain. The traditions are yet fresh of that terrible journey. A friend who has lived long in Salt Lake City told us of one poor woman who suffered fearfully from an internal ailment, but was whipped off if she ventured even to lay her hand on a waggon; and of another who lost the power of her limbs,

and had to be carried by one of her companions on her back.
All accounts testify to the Napoleon-like ability of Brigham
Young, controlling and directing not only this march, but
the whole operations of the colony, by his marvellous sagacity
and inflexible will.

But Utah and Salt Lake City must be reserved for another chapter.

CHAPTER IV.

SALT LAKE CITY AND THE MORMONS.

THE valley of Utah has been justly called an oasis in the desert. It is surrounded for the most part by lofty mountains, which seem to shut it out from the rest of the world; and for this reason the Mormons claim for their capital the divine protection which was signified by the mountains round about Jerusalem. It was in the hope of being left in peace to develop his peculiar institutions that Brigham Young chose this valley for the settlement of his people. But the construction of the Pacific Railway, which passes through the territory of Utah, put an end to their isolation, and brought them into the very highway of continental travel. When I was in this country nineteen years ago I met Mr. Colfax, then vice-President of the United States, and on my asking how the Government meant to deal with Mormonism, his reply to me was, "I guess the Pacific Railroad will pretty well settle that question." It is often boasted that Utah was but a desert when taken possession of, and that it is Mormon skill and labour that have turned it into a garden. But this is a great exaggeration. Being obviously the bed of an ancient lake, the plain has mostly a good soil, and it needed only cultivation and irrigation to make it productive. Idleness is strongly denounced by the Mormon authorities, and not wholly on disinterested grounds. One-tenth of the entire produce of every kind is remorselessly claimed by the Church, and idleness would not be a good contributor to the sustentation fund. The Mormons have certainly done well as farmers, but no better than the Gentiles in many other parts of the country.

The settlement was begun in 1847, and Salt Lake City dates from that time. It is now a city of 30,000 inhabitants, but nothing like Omaha or Denver. Brick and timber are nearly the only building materials, and even in the best streets wooden shanties are interspersed with tall brick erections in the way that shows that the stage has not been reached when taste asserts its claims as well as utility. The only remarkable buildings are the Tabernacle, the Assembly Hall, and the Temple—all adjacent. The Tabernacle is a huge, featureless building, like the back of a turtle or an oblong dish-cover: the profane call it "The Church of the Holy Turtle." It is said to be seated for 12,000. The Assembly Hall is a more architectural erection, and was designed for use in winter, when the congregations are smaller. The Temple is a huge structure, not yet completed, built, you might suppose, of Aberdeen granite, and when finished will be by far the most imposing edifice in all Utah. It is to be used for inaugurations, marriages, or other occasions to which the *profanum vulgus* are not admitted. It is an imposing structure, but wants harmony and repose, the parts cohering rather than forming a harmonious whole, and the general impression garish rather than venerable.

The population of Utah territory is about two hundred thousand, of whom some fifty thousand are "Gentiles," the rest Mormons. At first there were no Gentiles, and it is certainly not with the goodwill of the Mormons that they are now so numerous. A friend in New York, Dr. Ellinwood of the Presbyterian Mission Board, told me he had been three times in Utah. The first time he dared hardly to peep or mutter against Mormonism; the second time he had for a fellow-traveller Brigham Young's nineteenth wife on her way to the city to expose and denounce Mormonism; on the third he found the Christian Churches, represented by active organizations, doing a great amount of good.

Many causes have contributed to bring respectable Gentiles to Utah. Ogden, which stands a few miles to the north of Salt Lake City, is a great railway centre; there are many minerals in the territory which the saints cannot develop; some are always renouncing Mormonism; and the capabilities of the valley have attracted outside capitalists, who say, in American phrase, "there are millions in it." If the effort to be made at the elections next February shall succeed, Salt Lake will become, as Ogden has become, "an American city," the Mormons will be dispossessed of its government, and then its development is expected to go on very quickly. This consummation is not unlikely, for the recent action of the Federal Government has deprived all polygamists of the franchise, and a woman's suffrage that helped the Mormons greatly has been abolished. Moreover, there are many of the saints themselves who in their secret hearts would not regret a measure that would hasten the "boom" under which their property would perhaps double its value. One of the most outstanding and wealthy families of the city—the Walkers—are perverts from Mormonism. The Walker House is the best hotel in the place, and the Walker Store is a vast establishment. Old Mr. Walker, I am sorry to say, was a Scotsman, who turned Mormon; but being called on by Brigham Young to pay a tithe which he thought too high, he abandoned the connection. His sons, I believe, are all men of wealth and influence.

The Mormon creed is very skilfully constructed. It professes to conserve the whole Bible, the whole doctrines of Christianity, and the moral law. To this it adds, as if it were an innocent supplement, faith in the Book of Mormon, in the divine mission of Joe Smith, and in the doctrine that God continues to hold direct intercourse with the head of the Church, thus making him infallible, and making resistance to his orders an unpardonable sin against earth and heaven. The Mormon Government is ostensibly dual—namely, civil and ecclesiastical. But, in point of fact, the rulers of the Church are also the civil rulers and judges of the territory, and this makes their power enormous. Besides the president of the Church (at present Wilfrid Woodruff, a coarse-looking old man, with a most unspiritual face), there are twelve apostles, and a body of elders distributed over the whole Church. There are two hundred and seventy wards in the territory, each of which has its presiding officer; and the wards are subdivided into small districts, superintended in like manner. Thus it happens that the rulers of the Church have the most minute acquaintance with the affairs of every member. Every transaction of buying or selling, every cent of income, every dollar of profit is known, and a tenth must be most religiously paid to the Church, which thus becomes very rich. Nay, the president may announce that he has divine authority for demanding a man's house, or his land, or whatsoever he has. A woman may be told that she is to marry some fellow who already has a dozen wives. If she refuse, she cannot get to heaven. Into how many other matters of private life this system of tyranny has penetrated we cannot tell.

The Church has a supreme belief in her missionary function, and in her destiny as the centre of the Church of the future, when all the world shall be converted to Mormonism. Her characteristic hymns are full of this expectation, and no doubt many of her more ignorant people devoutly believe in it. She can requisition foreign missionaries, so many from every ward; and wherever these are sent, they must go at their own cost, and occupy themselves wholly in making converts. Usually they go about their work very quietly. Again and again I have heard it remarked as strange that so many Scotsmen are Mormons. But I do not wonder. They are not typical Scotsmen. The missionaries go about the slums of our cities, or our mining villages, express much concern for the hard conditions of labour, perhaps during a strike, then picture to them Utah as a land flowing with milk and honey, tell them their expenses will be paid out to the place (to be repaid afterwards), they will get fifteen or twenty acres free, and will rapidly rise to prosperity and wealth. They do not tell them that in other parts of the United States they may have a hundred and sixty acres free, without being subject to the appropriation of a tenth of the produce to the Church. To the religiously disposed they read from the English Bible, sing evangelical hymns, and leave the impression that Mormonism is a peculiarly devout form of Christianity. Often the converts have been told nothing of polygamy; and it is only after their arrival that they have found that neither their bodies nor their souls are their own. On the other hand, the Mormons have the character of being kind, neighbourly, and considerate towards one another; and every effort is made by the Church to stimulate the *esprit de corps*, and keep the sect united and hearty. Although the territory of Utah is their chief settlement, they are by no means confined to it. They have colonies in most of the Mountain States; and they are very astute in political matters, not attaching themselves formally to either party, but holding the balance between the two. The ablest man among them is said to be a Mr. Buchanan, who was their representative in the Senate, and who is extremely skilful in those wire-pulling operations that may conduce to their advantage.

But the political tide has been against them for some years, and is likely to be against them still more in the future. In 1862 Congress declared polygamy to be unlawful; but as there were neither judges nor juries disposed to enforce that law, it became only an example of the folly of laws which are not supported by the general sentiment of a people. It was not till 1882 that more decided steps were taken. The "Edmunds" law of that year was a very stringent one. A body of United States commissioners was appointed to settle the affairs of the territory; and there was established a military fort, Fort Douglass, with a detachment of United States troops, and artillery pointed at the great Mormon buildings, ready, in case of necessity, to reduce them to ruins. Since that time *open* polygamy has ceased to be known. Both polygamy and cohabitation with a plurality of women or *quasi* wives were declared criminal (the former having the severer penalty), and already some three hundred men have been committed to prison, mostly for the latter offence. Others have had to take to the "underground railway," or to commit their extra wives to its care—in other words, to hide. If you ask where Mr. So-and-So is, it is common to hear that he is "in the underground." The practice of *avowed* polygamy is now a tradition of the past. As you ride through Salt Lake City, you are shown the house where Brigham Young lived and died. Adjacent to it is his civil office, and next to it his ecclesiastical. Opposite is the Amelia Palace, a more handsome house, the abode of his favourite wife. Here and there are other houses which used to be occupied by other wives. One large house shows a long range of gables—one, it is said, for every wife that lived in it. In spite of the largeness of his family he died immensely rich. It does not appear that his sons or his daughters have come to honour.

The moral effect of the system is such as might be easily foreseen. Avowedly it was devised for the purpose of placing under regulation those tendencies which elsewhere lead to all manner of licentious irregularity. The hymns sung in worship contrast it triumphantly with such practices. But the effect has been the very opposite. What, indeed, can be the effect on young men when they see their father going off to San Francisco to visit one of his wives, or away to Nevada after another? *Mutatis mutandis*, they will follow his example. He claims for it the sanction of religion, but they see that there is precious little of religion about it; and if there be, it is a religion which they despise, so that very probably they become unbelievers. The whole relations of the sexes are thrown out of joint. Illegitimacy is said to be very common, but as the statistics are wholly in the hands of the Church, the facts are not known precisely. Profanity, falsehood, and similar vices abound. Many prosecutions for polygamy have broken down, because even where it was notorious, the witnesses swore the other way.

The scene within the Tabernacle on a Sunday afternoon is very striking. All the congregations meet in their parish churches in the morning; but in the afternoon there is a mass meeting in the Tabernacle, where they celebrate their communion. The galleries were unoccupied, but the vast area was filled. I should suppose there might be seven thousand present. One could not but be struck with the plainness of their appearance. They evidently belonged to the hard-working classes, and the less cultivated of them, for there was hardly an intellectual countenance among the whole. The rulers of the Church occupied benches on a platform, where the desk and books were placed. The services, as in other churches, were singing, prayer, preaching, and the communion. There were two preachers, both energetic and effective. Their sermons were apologetic, for there were seven hundred excursionists that day in the city, and many of these were present. I should rather have heard a sermon from the Book of Mormon, and exhortations such as one is told are often addressed to the peculiar people to keep them stanch and firm. The communion was a painful spectacle. Bread and water were handed round the immense audience, and partaken of with the utmost nonchalance, no token of reverence being apparent even on the benches occupied by apostles and elders. The children partook along with their parents, and were even obliged to do so. A poor child in front of me, tortured with ophthalmia, struggled hard to keep down her head, but her mother would not allow her, and shook her into compliance.

When I went to call on the Presbyterian minister, I found him occupying as his study an apartment which had formerly been occupied by one of the three wives of a polygamist. He took down four well-scored books from his shelves, and asked me if I knew them. Two of these were Mr. Stalker's books on the "Life of our Lord" and the "Life of St. Paul," for the latter of which he had an extraordinary appreciation. Another was the "Personal Life of David Livingstone," whom he regarded as the greatest missionary since St. Paul. The fourth was "The Public Ministry and Pastoral Methods of our Lord." I could not but express a strange pleasure at finding my books doing duty in the citadel of the Mormons. I told him that I had been disappointed that the book on our Lord's ministry, which I had thought would be a useful one, had fallen dead at home; but that I had found compensation for that disappointment in many testimonies I had received from ministers in the United States and professors of pastoral theology, including Dr. Hastings of Union Seminary, New York, and President Fisk of Chicago, to the interest with which they had read it. Dr. M'Niece (surely this must be a corruption of M'Niesh) occupies a good position and exercises an excellent influence. We attended his church on Sunday morning, and I preached for him in the evening. There was a second Presbyterian church in the city in the course of formation. Most of the Gentile churches seem to be in a vigorous state. These churches are doing good work also through their schools. The public schools and schoolbooks are pervaded by Mormonism. Denominational schools are inevitable, and they appear to be very efficient. One of these which I saw was a collegiate institution, under charge of the Presbyterian Church, admirably conducted, a sort of secondary school, with from two to three hundred young persons. Altogether from fifteen hundred to two thousand children are being taught in them, and I was informed that forty per cent. of these were of Mormon origin, but very likely to abandon the system altogether.

If polygamy dies out, will Mormonism survive? Possibly it will, and it may give no little trouble. The essence of Mormonism is that it is a priestly government, subordinating the political to the spiritual, and bringing to bear on its objects a power which is virtually that of spiritual infallibility. It has intrenched itself very strongly, has acquired great wealth, is very intolerant, and has inspired the mass of its people with a wonderful faith in the reality of its claims. Such a system will not easily pass away. Its mischievous influence may be perpetuated for a long time to come. It is like one of those noxious weeds that have their roots deep in the ground, and that are ever cropping up on every side, let the farmer do what he may.

A drive through Salt Lake City and its suburbs, including Fort Douglass, is exceedingly enjoyable. The ranges of snow-clad mountains that close in the view gleam brightly in the sunshine, and the green plain all around is full of tranquil beauty. Certainly "every prospect pleases—" Is it necessary to complete the couplet?

CHAPTER V.

THE YOSEMITE VALLEY.

LEAVING Salt Lake City on a Monday afternoon, we first had a glimpse of the Salt Lake itself. Fain would we have made a run to the fashionable watering-place on the Salt Lake, and had a dip in those waters which are more impregnated with salt than the Dead Sea, and equally destitute of fish, and which buoy one up so wonderfully that sinking in them is a kind of impossibility. We passed through Ogden, the second city of Utah, a railway junction, and likely to grow in population and importance. Then we committed ourselves to our sleeping-berths. Next morning we looked out on what proved a weary wilderness—the desert of Nevada.

Perhaps some readers may be interested to know a little of life in the cars. The cars are always like long rooms, with a passage running longitudinally, and seats holding two on either side. If two persons are travelling together, they usually get "a section" of the Pullman—that is, two seats which by day may be placed so that the occupants sit opposite to each other. As bedtime draws near, the porter, usually a coloured man, comes along and prepares the beds. First the two seats are drawn together, a mattress and other gear placed over them, and the lower bed prepared. Then, turning a screw, he folds down something like a broad shelf, attached by a hinge to the sloping roof of the car, and this, with bed-gear corresponding, forms the upper bed. Curtains are then attached to a rod that runs along the top of the car, closing in both beds, and the process is complete. You smuggle yourself somehow into bed, and divest yourself of your clothing as best you may. It is not an easy process, for the roof is very low. In the morning you are probably awakened by the porter calling out, "Breakfast in half-an-hour." You know that that is an announcement not to be trifled with. You wriggle hastily into your clothes, jump up, then move along to the end of the car, where there is a lavatory with a very small basin; and waiting your turn, you get your face and hands dipped and cleansed. Ladies are better off; they have a little room. Returning to your berth, you move through the narrow avenue, amid shoulders, elbows, and knees bulging out against the curtains, representing the contortions of your belated fellow-travellers who are yet struggling to get inside their garments. The porter is already busy "fixing" the vacated berths. It may be that your breakfast is at a roadside station, and in that case you leave the car. But it may also be that there is no hotel or restaurant for hundreds of miles; in these circumstances a "dining-car" is hooked on to the train, and you pass along to it for your meal. The fare is wonderfully good, and by no means cheap; but often the car sways about so vehemently that eating is far from pleasant. The hours of the day pass wearily to some, and the pack of cards—symbol so often of poor resources elsewhere—is produced very early. For the victims of tobacco, there is a small smoking room, generally in good demand. Those who eschew both cards and tobacco, when they tire of their book will find their fellow-passengers very willing for conversation; or, if they want fresh air, may stand a little on the platform at the end of the car. Where there is varied and beautiful scenery, and the smoke is not blown in your face, this is delightful; but where there is nothing but wilderness, the attraction is small.

And wilderness it was all that day, as we moved through the state of Nevada. We were not sorry when night came on and we betook ourselves again to our sleeping-berths. When we got up next morning, we were close to Sacramento, the state capital of California. The scene had undergone a delightful change. We were among groves of greenery, and saw for the first time the orange-tree in its native clime, luxuriating in the sunshine and loaded with its apples of gold. We could not but recall lines written of another land, " far, far away":—

> " Know ye the land of the cedar and vine,
> Where the flowers ever blossom, the beams ever shine;
> Where the light wings of zephyr, oppressed with perfume,
> Wax faint o'er the gardens of Gúl [the rose] in her bloom;
> Where the citron and olive are fairest of fruit,
> And the voice of the nightingale never is mute;
> Where the tints of the earth and the hues of the sky,
> In colour though varied, in beauty may vie,
> And the purple of ocean is deepest in dye?"

We had an hour to spend in Sacramento, and by the aid of the street car we were soon among its lions. Its Capitol is very handsome, a kind of miniature of that of Washington, and the Roman Catholic cathedral is massive and stately. In other respects the city is ordinary enough. It finds it too hard to compete with San Francisco, and, wisely, it does not try.

Our plan was to defer our visit to San Francisco until our return journey, and spend that week in the Yosemité Valley. We were still in flowery May, and if we had deferred the Yosemité trip we should have found the flowers all gone and the waterfalls all dry. Though we hardly knew what we were to encounter, we were very thankful that we made this arrangement, for we had an admirable opportunity of seeing the valley.

Lying in the heart of the Sierra Nevada, the Yosemité Valley is one of the most remarkable and interesting bits of American scenery. It is reached most easily, if the word easily may be used in such a connection, from the station of Berenda, on the Southern Pacific Railway, about a hundred miles from San Francisco on the north, and between three and four hundred from Los Angeles on the south. The service of trains on that line is very limited; for though we arrived at Berenda at four in the afternoon, there was no means of getting further till five next morning. Berenda is one of those stations in the midst of the wilderness where art seems to have vied with nature to make the place the very climax of desolation; for with all its gorgeous beauty in many parts, California is but a waste, howling wilderness in others. For accommodation in a wretched hotel you pay at the same rate as in the best of the country; and indeed you may reckon as the usual charge all the time you are in the valley a dollar a meal and a dollar a bed, save in one or two instances where you get a rapid meal for three-quarters. The charge for conveyance is also high: "the round" from Berenda and back is forty-five dollars; and if to the hotel charges you add something for a carriage drive here, or a saddle horse there, you will find that a week in the Yosemité costs for each person not much under twenty pounds.

At five in the morning you go on board the cars on a branch railway, and in an hour and a half you are carried to Raymond, where the tug-of-war, in the form of stage-coach fighting with the mountain passes, begins. After breakfast you are allocated to a place in one of the stage-coaches (of which there may be half-a-dozen); and as there was a party of the name of Stewart from Los Angeles, and two of the seats in their stage were not required by them, the clerk seems to have thought that the couple from Scotland might find fittest accommodation there. A most agreeable party it was, and the easy and kindly manners of California enabled the people from the old country very soon to feel themselves at home.

Before starting on the stage we were already pretty high up among the mountains, for the railway has the steepest gradient in California, and does its very best to carry us up. And we were in a very different scene from that which we left at Berenda. The weary sage-brush which dots the wilderness with awful monotony had entirely disappeared, and we were already in the region of most beautiful trees and flowers. This, perhaps, is the first feature that strikes the stranger. You see in the woods flowering trees covered with blossoms, as if they were huge rose bushes in full bloom; while at your feet you have masses of flowers, pink, blue, purple, scarlet, as if the blaze of Dirleton garden had been scattered over acres and miles. You have only to get down as the horses are changed, and in five minutes you have gathered a bouquet fit for a bride. And yet I do not know that the effect is more pleasing than that of our own laburnums, chestnuts, and hawthorn, and charming banks and meadows of daisy, primrose, and buttercup. The distance you have to travel the first day (to Wawona) is about forty miles, but it occupies the whole day till nightfall. We had five changes of horses during the day, so that in all twenty horses were needed to haul eleven persons along. The lower ranges of the Sierra Nevada are striking and beautiful. The outlines of the hills, and the far-reaching glimpses one gets from time to time, remind one of the Grampians near Blair Athole, while the rich clothing of pine and oak and other trees seems to recall the scenery of Dunkeld. The whole was set forth to perfection by the brightest sun that ever shone and the purest sky that ever gleamed. The effect of the climate was wonderfully invigorating; the party were all in the best of spirits, entering with all their hearts into the beauty of the scene. The only drawbacks were the excessive heat and the excessive dust, of both of which we may truly say that it was impossible to contend with them; the only alternative was to submit as gracefully as possible to their absolute control.

As we got more into the heart of the mountains, the trees became more striking. We were not yet among *the* big trees, but we were among bigger trees than we had ever seen. Very striking was the aspect of the ordinary pine-trees, especially as they rose from the valleys, some two hundred feet in height, pointing to heaven as straight as arrows, and displaying in branches and leafage the most perfect symmetry. It seemed hardly possible for any one to escape the moral lesson—it would be well for us if we rose to heaven as straight and direct as these noble trees.

American forest roads are not perfection. But the wonder is that in such a region of hill and valley there are carriage-roads at all. In few cases has more been done than to clear a path; and often the ruts remind you of the entrance to a stone-quarry, or the track formed by cart-wheels in excavating the foundations of a house. While the coach ascends, the movement is very slow, but it is safe and comfortable; but woe betide you when it plunges downhill, determined to make up for time lost in the ascent! Let no lady or other mortal dream of attempting this journey who cannot stand being knocked and tossed hither and thither, especially when the coach strikes on a stone or a concealed row of logs, and bumps you up and down half-a-dozen times in succession, as if you were dancing a jig. For this same movement must be undergone for several days, and for delicate ladies it is certainly too much.

Evening brings you to the hotel at Wawona. You are still half a day's journey from the Yosemité Valley, but you are comparatively near the celebrated "big trees," and it is convenient to visit them from this place. Wawona in the native tongue means "big trees." The distance to and from is but seventeen miles, but it occupies about four or five hours. As you penetrate into the forest you observe, in addition to the tall pines and arbor vitæ to which you have been accustomed, a new variety, of unprecedented thickness, and bright russet stems, having a look of very hoary antiquity. It is the tree known among us but as a shrub, the *Wellingtonia gigantea*, as we call it, but the *Washingtonia gigantea* of the Americans. Both of these names, however, bid fair to be superseded by the term *Siquoia gigantea*, applied by a recent Government botanist, who observed that this was but a variety of the big redwood trees of the coast, to which the name *Siquoia sempervirens* had already been given. In these mountains this tree grows to a size unprecedented in any other part of the globe. It is a clannish tree, and even here is found only in certain bits of the forest. How it comes to grow here to such prodigious proportions we cannot tell, except that the soil, the climate, and the shelter of the Mariposa county must be highly favourable to its growth.

The more striking trees have got peculiar names, appropriate to their appearance. There is the Grizzly Giant, the Three Graces, the Graceful Couple, Uncle Tom's Cabin, and the like. The thickest tree in the grove is the Grizzly Giant. Some young persons brought a ball of twine and put it round him. They included a projecting root which they should have omitted; this made the length of the piece of twine between thirty and forty yards. Another tree has a passage scooped out at the root, through which the stage-coach with its four horses easily passes; but this tunnel seems in no degree to interfere with the welfare of the tree. Near where we stopped to rest our horses occurs a remarkable prostrate tree. It is some three hundred feet long. It is so high that a ladder is needed for you to get on it, and the first hundred feet might be scooped out to form a considerable ship. The rest of the tree contained timber more than enough to stock a large timber-yard. It is no myth that is told of a farmer who had acquired a hundred and sixty acres of land, that out of one tree he got timber enough to build his house and barns, and to enclose the whole of his farm, and had a large quantity over for such other purposes as he required it. A tree on the border of a county so fell that while its root was in one county its stem was in another. The number of such stories told of the big trees is very great.

Next morning we bid farewell for a time to Wawona, which is charmingly situated in an amphitheatre of hills, with a clear rapid stream flowing past. With our stage and four horses we penetrated still further into the Sierra. Up the steep ascents, in which we had occasionally to double upon ourselves, our rate of progress was sometimes not more than three miles an hour, and often we had to pause to give the poor horses their breath. Every here and there we would reach a commanding point, from which we looked out on a scene of wonderful sylvan beauty. One of these is named "Oh My Point," because no American can look out from it without indulging his characteristic exclamation, "Oh my!" At last, about mid-day, we reached the far-famed "Inspiration Point," and paused to look down on the glories of Yosemité. It is a very striking view. About ten or twelve miles of narrow valley spread out before us, enclosed in abrupt almost perpendicular mountains, rising to the height of some four thousand feet, broken at the summits into every variety of picturesque form, and gleaming with silver streaks of waterfalls so steep that the water is dashed to spray long before it reaches the bottom, and when the sun is behind the spectator, shines in the tints of the rainbow. Inspiration Point commands a splendid view of El Capitan, the boldest of the cliffs, and the Bridal Veil, perhaps the finest of the waterfalls.

As we move downwards, and get into the valley, its other fine features appear. Among the most striking of these are Sentinel Cliff, Cathedral Spires, the Three Brothers, the Three Graces, the Half Dome, and the North Dome. Cathedral Spires is the name of two pointed spires that rise six or seven hundred feet above the general summit, having a striking resemblance to the object from which they derive their name. The Half Dome is a huge mass of dome-shaped rock, that in some convulsion of nature has been split in two, leaving the question a puzzle for mankind—What became of the other half? But of all the rocks El Capitan is the most wonderful. He rises in almost sheer perpendicular height three thousand three hundred feet, with corresponding breadth, and so far as you can see there is not a seam or division in the vast mass of granite. Of the waterfalls, the Bridal Veil (the name explains itself) is sweet and beautiful, but the Nevada Falls have more variety of form and a larger mass of water. Everywhere the pine is at home. It often finds for itself a home in the very face of the rocks, or crowns their very summits.

Seen from any commanding point, under the bluest of skies and the brightest of sunshine, the valley is wonderfully grand. The surface is level and very rich, evidently the bottom of a lake in former times. But the glorious amphitheatre of nearly perpendicular rocks is what makes it so unique and so sublime. It is really something for Americans to be proud of, and in all likelihood it is unexampled in the world. Yet I must confess I like some of the Swiss valleys better. Amid all the grandeur of Yosemité, there is a want of that softness of beauty which sets off so well the sublimities of the Alps. And we want the snowy summits piercing the heavens and mingling with them, and speaking to us so expressively of the union of earth and heaven. But mass and magnitude are very expressive to the American mind, and I have no doubt that those who have travelled far are sincere in declaring, as they often do most enthusiastically, that there is nothing like the Yosemité in all the world.

There are two hotels in the valley—Barnard's and the Stoneman House. We were recommended to take the former, which is also the older, and we were glad that we did so. It is charmingly situated, and our bedroom window, and the veranda on which it opened, commanded a delightful view of the Yosemité Fall, a cascade in three leaps, the tallest of which is some fifteen hundred feet, and the whole, I think, about two thousand six hundred. Nothing could be more charming than to sit in the evening and gaze on the stream of virgin silver losing itself in foam, but quickly pulling itself together for another leap. We had the pleasure to be much in contact with Mr. M'Cord, the guardian or Government official of the valley, and to receive from him much information and attention. We were happy to be able to repay him in some degree by taking the Sunday service in the chapel, of which he takes charge. We must mention another inhabitant, Mr. Galen Clark, the discoverer of the big trees, a man full of intelligence and scientific knowledge, and whom, after all he has done for the valley, it is a pain to see living alone in his old age, and earning a humble living by hiring a carriage for the use of visitors. [Hardly had I written these lines when the political whirligig brought a rapid change. Mr. M'Cord was sent adrift, and Mr. Clark appointed guardian. As in most cases in America, politics did it. We were glad that Mr. Clark was promoted, but vexed for Mr. M'Cord.]

The Stoneman House, a mile and a quarter further up the valley, is a large three-storied building, named after some Governor Stoneman, but is much less fortunate in its situation than Barnard's. There are several weeks in winter when the sun can be seen for little more than an hour. But here, as elsewhere, people complain of the way in which things are done by the authorities. The valley is the property of the United States, but is under the charge of the state of California, who appoint a body of commissioners to look after it. These commissioners will pay it a visit now and then, and on one of these occasions they resolved to build this Stoneman Hotel, without having consultation with the few residents, and without being aware of the strong objections to the situation.

The history of the valley is not uninteresting. During the whole period of the Spanish occupation of California it seems to have been unknown. It was in a somewhat accidental way that it was discovered by the Americans in the early days of the gold enterprise. The county of Mariposa, in which both the valley and the big trees are situated, has some valuable gold mines. The miners were ever and anon having depredations committed on them by Indians, whose whereabouts could not be discovered. At length it was found that their home was in a valley to which all access was impossible save at one or two points, which they carefully guarded. War ensued, and it ended in the Indians being dispossessed. There is a dispute whether the true name of the valley, which in the Indian language is said to mean, "The home of the grizzly bear," ought to be Yosemité or Yohamité. Usage has settled the question in favour of the former, but it is apt to suggest the idea of Shem dwelling in the tents of Ham. For a few years after the discovery of the valley it remained unfrequented. A gentleman who was about to publish a work on "Picturesque California" remembered that he had heard of a waterfall in the valley eight hundred feet high. He determined to find it and insert it in his work. With two companions he set out on the search. He gives an amusing account of his efforts to find some of the men who had taken part in the military operations, but one after another had forgot all about the way to the place, only each was sure such another could tell it. After going for a long time from post to pillar, Mr. Hutchings at last found the way into the valley, and then discovered scenes that threw all other parts of "Picturesque California" into the shade.

The permanent residents in the valley are hardly a score in number, but in summer it swarms with visitors, and it is not the hotels only that shelter them. "Camping out" is a common operation. A family, or a cluster of families, pitch a tent in the valley, travel in their own buggy or waggon, bring with them cooking utensils, and manage to have a very "good time" for a week or longer. The camping-ground being near the hotels, I happened to pass an encampment of this sort on the Sunday afternoon, when I was immediately accosted by a gentleman, who introduced himself as a professor of mathematics in Massachusetts, sojourning in California for his health. He had just been preparing notes of my sermon for the local paper, and wished to read them over to me. "The local paper," I said; "what do you mean?" "Oh, there's a printer in camp here, who brought with him a printing machine and set of types, and every week he prints the *Yosemité Gazette*." Most thoroughly American! Americans can make newspapers live where there seems as little to live on as for the pines on the face of the rock. And sometimes there are two rival papers where there is hardly a decent house. And these can abuse each other as roundly as the famous newspapers of Eatanswill. The newspaper is a wonderful institution in America.

On the following day we had a pleasant drive in Mr. Clark's conveyance, first to the Mirror Lake, and thereafter all down and up the valley. The effects of the tossing in the stage-coaches prevented one of our party from attempting more. But some of the waterfalls I reached on foot. It was interesting to look over the official list of visitors in the guardian's book. Among the earliest was Charles Kingsley, whose name was entered without note or comment. Known names occurred from time to time. The latest name of all was that of a family from Edinburgh, of whose existence I had never heard.

Of the glacial condition of the valley and of the Sierra Nevada at one period there seems to be no doubt. But how these mighty masses of rock came into their present position no mortal can tell. The impression one is apt to have is, that at one time the opposite sides met, and that they were severed by some unexampled explosive force that tossed them asunder as if they were the playthings of a child. Anyhow, they form now the Titanic battlements of a valley which well repays the visit of the tourist. Nowhere does nature appear greater, or man more feeble and dependent. And yet man continues to subdue even this valley to his purposes. A railway has already been surveyed between Raymond and Wawona, and we shall be much surprised if American enterprise does not succeed ultimately in carrying the rails into the valley itself, and thereafter in laying a mountain line, hardly, indeed, to the summit of El Capitan, but possibly to the Glacier Point, or some other eminence that commands the whole.

CHAPTER VI.

LOS ANGELES.

ON our return journey we again spent a night and part of two days at Wawona. From Wawona to Raymond we had a very lively ride. Not only had we lively company, but we had a remarkable coachman. A theological topic started in conversation set him off at the nail. He not only understood theology, but he knew the Bible, and he could give his objections to current theological dogmas with great felicity and force. There was more than one clergyman beside him, and laymen who were quite *au fait* in the discussion; but he spoke as well as any of them, and, without being offensive, with all that self-possession and self-respect which Americans feel in talking to persons who (according to our notion) are socially above them. Some one tried to give a practical turn to the discussion by dropping a remark about minding the life to come. "It's not easy to mind the life to come," he said, "and drive a stage." He said this in a regretful tone. He had no Sabbath and no church, and those among whom he lived were in the same predicament. The mystery of his controversial power was solved when we learned that he had been a Baptist minister, but had abandoned that calling. In the States ex-clergymen have often to resort to strange occupations. But this is infinitely less thought of there than it would be with us.

And really these coachmen have a difficult task; but they seemed all steady and capable men. There are hundreds of places where want of care and vigilance might overturn the coach and cost many lives. A combination of dash and caution is needed, which does not often occur. I could not help recalling an incident in my visit to the White Mountains nine years before. My wife and daughter had gone with me in the railway to the top of Mount Washington, where we spent the night. Next morning my daughter and I decided to descend on foot, while the elder lady took a place on the stage. After the coach passed us pedestrians, and we saw the break-neck precipices along which it had frequently to go, we became somewhat alarmed about its safety. I comforted myself with the thought that I had seen no place on Mount Washington where the driver could have got drink, and that therefore he could not but be sober. We "forgathered" with an American gentleman who knew the road well. At a turn of it, in a wood, I observed a strange gap and signs of smash-up among the trees. "Do you know the cause of that?" I asked. "Yes, sir. The coach was upset there a month ago, and the coachman and one of the passengers were killed." "But how could the coach be upset in such a place?" "I believe, sir, *the man was drunk!*"

At Raymond we had our third meal. You may call the meals breakfast, dinner, and tea or supper if you like, but really they are pretty much the same, and to us they were rather much of a good thing. In one of our journeys afterwards we sympathized with the remark of an eminent medical gentleman, who, like ourselves, had omitted the middle meal, "I cannot eat three dinners a day."

From Raymond again to Berenda in the train. Another long wait at Berenda, from dusk to four o'clock next morning; but instead of revisiting the hotel, we took sleeping-berths in a car. When the south-going train from San Francisco caught us up, we were carried at first over a fairly-cultivated but not very interesting country; but as the forenoon wore on, it became more and more desolate, and at last culminated in the great Mojavé desert. We travelled through the great central valley of California, with the range of the Sierra Nevada on our left and the Coast Range on our right. Near what is called "The Loop," the one range has a crossing to the other, and the railway has to make another memorable climb. It turns upon itself, buries itself in tunnels, reverses its direction, bewilders you as you try to find your bearings, and does all the other funny things a railway must do when it cannot get a level to run on. To us the idea of danger hardly suggested itself; but it is not long since a train going down escaped from the control of the breaks, and was dashed over a precipice at a fearful speed, causing many deaths and mutilations, and that, too, in the darkness of night. The mountains through which we passed were often beautiful in form, but naked and dry, and therefore less interesting. We were suddenly startled from our languor by coming on some beautiful specimens in full flower of the *Yucca gloriosa*, known among the people as the Spanish bayonet. They towered up, the stem ten or twelve feet in height, while the pure white bells clung to the stem in hundreds, full-formed and perfect in symmetry. Soon after, we came on a great hill-side swarming with them from top to bottom. And now and again we had patches of them for many miles till we got near Los Angeles.

Seventy miles from Los Angeles we passed Lancaster, a place of which we had often heard from one who had made trial of it, but had been forced to leave it because it had no water. The little village with its two or three dozen houses appeared to us raw enough, and the country bleak enough; nevertheless it maintained two weekly newspapers, of one of which we possessed ourselves, and found it rather at a loss for topics, except when it had occasion to pound away at its rival. Then we passed through a prettier valley, and at seven o'clock we reached Los Angeles. The railway station had been moved, just a little before, from the near to the far end of the town; but in America railways have no scruple running along the streets, without fence or guard, counting it enough to ring a bell—an arrangement which may do well enough in the daytime, but is sometimes very disastrous by night. As we moved along we had a good view of the older part of Los Angeles, and also of its Chinatown, the Chinese hieroglyphics and strange names, "Ling Lung Lee's Laundry," "Wun Lung," and what not, being new to us, and therefore interesting.

Before speaking of the city, it will be well to go back a little and glance at the history of the country. It needs to be remembered that California is a very large state, and that the whole of California is not in the state. The most southerly part, known as Lower California, is still part of Mexico. But even American California is equal in area to eight other states combined, and some of them big ones —New York, New Jersey, Massachusetts, Vermont, Maine, New Hampshire, Connecticut, and Ohio. If it were asked what its size is relative to Great Britain, I should be reminded of a remark of my friend, George H. Stuart of Philadelphia, when presiding some years ago at a meeting in Paris held to commemorate the success of the Bible kiosk at one of the Exhibitions. He began by remarking that he came from America; that America was a very large country, much larger than England, much larger even than France—all which remarks (except the last) were well received. It is so big, he continued, that if you cut the area of France and England out of it, it would never be missed. The translator fancied his meaning to be that America was so great a country that if you blotted England and France out of existence they would never be missed, and he sternly refused to translate so atrocious a remark! But it is literally true that the area of England might be cut out of California, and if you cut it out of the mountainous and desert tracts, it would hardly be missed.

In the distant past California was peopled thinly enough by a race respecting the origin of which our learned men are much puzzled. Humboldt reckoned the population in his day at fifteen thousand five hundred natives and thirteen hundred of other races. It comes into the sphere of history in the days of the Spanish occupation. The most notable fact connected with that period is the mission of Jesuit fathers, undertaken with a view to the conversion of the natives to Christianity. But Spain fell out with the Jesuits, who were expelled from all her borders, and the California mission was transferred to the Franciscans. How little permanent mark the original inhabitants left on the country is apparent from the fact that almost everywhere, at least in Southern California, the native names of places have given way to those introduced by the mission fathers. There is hardly a place but bears the name of some saint or saintess. San Francisco is named after the great founder of the order, and San Diego, San Pedro, San Gabriel, Santa Paula, Santa Barbara, Santa Anna, Santa Monica, and a hundred more, are all taken from the calendar. Certainly if sacred names could make a sacred land, California should be a holy country. As for Los Angeles, it was judged too heavenly a place to bear the name of any mere saint. Its full name is said to be "La Ciudad de la Reina de los Angeles"—the city of the queen of the angels. This, however, is shortened into Los Angeles. According to the Spanish pronunciation, which the older inhabitants retain, the "o" in Los is sounded distinctly, but not too long; "ang" is sounded as in angle, and with a nasal intonation as in Spanish. The old native name was Yang Na, and the river on which it is situated, now also called the Los Angeles, was Porcuincula. Under the mission fathers the country was but little changed. The natives came to profess Christianity of a sort, but remained little civilized. The fathers introduced good breeds of sheep, oxen, and horses on the hills, and near the villages the grape and other fruit trees; and to this day a kind of grape, excellent for wine but not for raisins, is called the mission-grape. Of late years, however, a strange blight has fallen upon the whole of this species, and it looks as if it would be exterminated.

Then came the time, early in this century, when Mexico revolted from Spain and set up for itself. California was in turn a department of the Mexican empire and a province in the Mexican republic. And during this period the Mexican Government came down heavily on the missions. These missions had got possession of large and valuable lands. The Mexican Government secularized a great part of them. The missions were reduced to comparative poverty, and now they are insignificant factors in the history of the country. Now, also, although there are some families of pure Spanish blood, the Spaniards and the aborigines have got mixed together. They form a mixed race, usually called Mexicans, who forty years ago were the chief inhabitants of the country, but are now almost buried under the Anglo-Saxon invasion.

More than forty years ago the United States were at war with Mexico. The dispute arose about Texas, which, before joining the Union, had been Mexican territory. In 1848, when the war was brought to a close, California was ceded to the States on their paying fifteen million dollars, and taking over debts of three or four millions more. Mexico was not able to hold it, and once there was some word of its passing into the hands of Great Britain. But the American

Government was desirous to have a hold on the Pacific coast, and on this account bought the country, little dreaming what a valuable possession they would be found to have obtained when the resources of California should be laid bare.

Up to this time the visits of the Anglo-Saxon to California had been few and far between. The adventurous fur-trader or the daring sportsman might occasionally cross the Rocky Mountains, or the hardy sailor from the isthmus of Panama might anchor in the bay of San Diego or of San Francisco; and, more rarely, the agriculturist might acquire a ranch and devote himself to the breeding of cattle. After the country became American, many Mexicans were ready to dispose of their ranches and move southwards to what still remained Mexican soil. More American settlers thus came to California. The discovery of gold at Sutter Mills, in the north, the year after it was ceded to America, brought a vast mass of people to the northern part of the state, mongrel enough in many ways, but all with a raging gold-hunger. To Southern California the steps of a quieter race of settlers were directed by the cheapness of land which Mexican owners were willing to dispose of. There are traditions that these American settlers behaved very cruelly and unjustly to the Mexican owners. Tales of flagrant wrong and cruel eviction were everywhere in Mexican mouths. I have been told that this may partly be accounted for by the fact that the Mexicans, who were an easy-going people and careless financiers, would borrow money on mortgage over their properties, and failing to pay interest, became legally liable to the loss of their property, of which the lender took possession. But we all know that under colour of law there may be great injustice done in this way to the poor and helpless, and it is quite likely that Mexicans suffered bitterly. A novel called "Ramona," which has been very extensively read, has for its object to expose the cruel wrongs which were inflicted on the original inhabitants. It is a powerfully-written romance, and one feels that if the half of it be true the Mexicans must have had hard lines.

And now, as we have said, the Mexicans are hardly an appreciable part of the population. There are yet settlements of them, as at San Gabriel, near Los Angeles, the oldest of the mission stations; and if one desires to see Mexicanism in full play, to study the Mexican face and character, or to examine the old Mexican church, and sundry other memorials of the olden time, let him bend his footsteps thither. But the Mexicans were not a vigorous race. They just dodged along. Many of them had joined the vices of Spain to their own. When Los Angeles was a Mexican town (which it was less than twenty years ago), its tastes were low and its manners rowdy. Sunday was the great day for jollity and revelry. If an American should show himself on the streets, he was liable to be surrounded by Mexicans threatening to shoot him if he did not take them into a saloon and treat them.

Though California is all one state to-day, it seems very likely that, like Dakota, it will one day be cut in two. It is inconvenient to have the capital, Sacramento, five hundred miles distant from San Diego, the most southern town. And, really, the two parts of the state are sufficiently diverse to call for separation. The great features of Southern California are its fruit and its climate. In both of these respects it surpasses the north. It draws to itself a class of people of a somewhat different type. The seven counties reckoned to Southern California have an area of above fifty-six thousand square miles, and an estimated population of three hundred and twelve thousand. The other day the county of Los Angeles was divided, and a new county, Orange— a suggestive name—was made out of it. Here is the area and the population of the seven counties:—

Counties.	Square Miles.	Population.
San Luis Obispo	3,578	20,000
Kern	8,100	10,000
Santa Barbara	2,265	25,000
Ventura	1,682	12,000
Los Angeles	4,812	165,000
San Bernardino	21,171	30,000
San Diego	14,968	50,000

The population is sufficient for a state, and there is spirit enough in Los Angeles to aspire to the distinction. But I suppose that when that dignity is obtained not a little expense must be incurred in the erection of a State House and all the rest of it; and as the present times are not very prosperous financially, it seems prudent in the southerners to delay proceedings in that direction.

Los Angeles has a fine situation. It is built on heights rising from the Los Angeles river, street rising above street; and while some of the suburbs spread over spacious meadows, others, as is indicated in such names as Angelina Heights, Boyle Heights, etc., straggle over gentle hills, while the horizon is splendidly bounded by a high, picturesque mountain-range. The city itself is more than a hundred years old; but as a thing of life, its origin is within the last twenty. So late as 1880 its population was only twelve thousand; now it is variously reckoned at from fifty thousand to eighty thousand. Its rapid rise was due to an extraordinary "boom" about three years ago, which came on the place like a great epidemic, and for the time being afflicted the whole people with a speculative madness. It was not the first "boom," however. I was told by an old inhabitant (that is, one who had been there about a dozen years) that soon after he came there was a similar "boom," which seemed likely to "boom" the place out of existence. The reaction was very serious: the principal bank failed; many of the leading people failed; and the state of Arizona coming into notice, with its mineral treasures, seemed likely to drain the place of all its people. But Los Angeles picked itself up again even after that disaster, and it has not gone down in any such way after the recent "boom." There have not been many failures; the price of real estate, though lower, shows no plunge downwards; and many buildings and other operations are going on that indicate a steady progressive movement.

There is still enough to show what the old Mexican city was like, stretching along a single line of unpaved, unlighted street, with its one-storied *adobé* cottages, and its long, low-roofed, very plain Roman Catholic church. I made it a business to find out the oldest American inhabitant who had been born in the city. I think I discovered this interesting object in the person of a young married lady of twenty-five. She remembered quite well the little Mexican city with but one two-storied house. One thing that contributed in a considerable degree to the rapid improvement of the place was the ambition of leading citizens to rear "blocks," called after their name, that would rival, if not eclipse, all that their neighbours had built. You have the Temple Block and the Nadeau Block, and all manner of other blocks. And a fine city they have made of it. It has quite a character of its own—is not a mere little Chicago, or a lesser San Francisco, but just itself. Probably the finest feature is the suburbs. Villas shaded by leafy groves, or adorned by palms and bananas, with bright green lawns kept verdant by the daily play of the hose, greet you in many directions. You see a greater regard to taste than in many new cities of America, and more respect to the *tout ensemble*, to a certain harmony of the parts, though, of course, this last is not easily realized.

Two or three of the subordinate features of Los Angeles are well worth attention. One is the street cars. Except in the case of San Francisco, I have seen no town with such a service of cable-cars. And cable-cars, when they are safe, are far the nicest. No smoke or smell of engine, no sight of panting and smoking horses, no slow, wearied pull uphill, or sound of hissing brake as you go down, ever distresses you. You travel as fast up the steepest hill as on level ground, and it makes no difference whether the car be empty, or the very platform be so crowded as to double the natural number of passengers. Los Angeles is beautifully and plentifully served with cars of various sorts—horse-cars, donkey-cars, mule-cars—in every direction. When I was there, a company, said to consist of Chicago gentlemen, had just expended two million dollars in cable-lines—a proof that they had confidence in the growing prosperity of the city. Then there is the telephone system. The multitude of wires overhead reminds one of Chicago or New York, except that in New York they are now laying the wires underground. In fact, as we passed through New York we witnessed a somewhat difficult operation—the hewing down of telephone-posts, calling to one's mind the early days when clearing away the forests was the first step of civilization. And lastly, the electric-lighting of the city. This is splendidly done, and at no little cost. The lights surmount huge poles, that look like the masts of a man-of-war, and must have been furnished from the matchless forests of Mariposa or Oregon. At night you see them at the distance of many miles with a lustre that eclipses stars of the first magnitude, and makes you think what a blessing it would be if the light of truth and holiness streamed forth from Los Angeles with corresponding brightness.

And this brings me to the Churches. There are no very imposing church buildings, but in the newer erections (all are of wood) there is manifest improvement. I had the pleasure of becoming acquainted with most of the leading clergy, and found them to be earnest men, for the most part lively preachers, and with catholic hearts. There is no little vigour, too, in the undertakings which flow out of the Churches. The Young Men's Christian Association has just entered a large and very handsome building. There is a feeling prevalent among American gentlemen of influence that this is a proper and necessary adjunct of a large city, and out of a kind of national pride, as well as from higher motives, they are ready to contribute much larger sums for this purpose than our people give. Then there is a very handsome temperance temple. There are missions to the Chinese carried on by the Churches with a fair measure of success, and some of the Chinese are members of the ordinary congregations of the city. There is no little activity on the part of the Christian women in various directions. The prayer-meetings are much better attended than with us. The first meeting I attended was the week-night prayer-meeting of the First Presbyterian Church, when there were nearly two hundred present. I observed that most of the office-bearers were present, and a full choir. The meeting was warm and cordial.

The provision for education in California is excellent. The school buildings are large and handsome, and fitted up, as is usual in America, in a much more comfortable style than is usual in our country. The education, as every one knows, is free, and even the advanced classes are attended by both sexes alike. The salaries of teachers and assistants range from some three thousand dollars to one thousand. The schools were in vacation most of the time I was in the country, but I had some opportunities of seeing the work. I was much struck with the quiet orderliness of the classes, and especially with the great skill of some of the female teachers teaching Greek or mathematics, and the profound respect with which they were listened to even by moustached young men.

In Southern California not much has been done as yet for university education. The foremost body in this department are the Methodists. They have been working for some years at "The University of Southern California." They have reared colleges in five or six different places, united into a university. For example, they have an agricultural college at Ontario. They have a theological college, if I remember rightly, at San Diego. Their department of arts and literature is in the suburbs of Los Angeles. I had the pleasure of being invited to the trustees' meeting, and of being asked to address a large assemblage in the hall of the university. Of students, the female part seemed considerably to outnumber the male. Among others whom I had the pleasure of meeting on that occasion was a very distinguished man, now well-stricken in years, General John C. Fremont, who many years before was employed by the Government to make the first survey of the region of the Rocky Mountains and all the country to the west. The results of this undertaking are given in two large quarto volumes, in the form of the General's Life; a work full of interest, but rather long for the general reader. Fremont had an active part, too, in the Mexican war, and I think he fell under censure, not for lack of service, but for the very opposite reason. He was of a daring and independent spirit, and somewhat like Lord Nelson when he put the telescope to his blind eye and declared he could not see the signal! His wife shared his love of enterprise, though his expedition separated her from him almost immediately after their marriage. There is a story that, after he was appointed, and when all his arrangements had been made, there came a letter from Government recalling the expedition. His wife opened the letter, and, seeing what it was, took care not to let him have it till several days after he had set out, so that he could tell the Government with a good conscience that he had not got their letter till it was too late!

I cannot say a great deal for the newspapers of Los Angeles. There are four daily and some weekly papers. They are very loyal to their city, and do their best to promote its material welfare; but there is too much of the sensational in them. Robberies, murders, and scandals are too conspicuous. A tone of exaggeration marks the narratives, making it difficult to rely on the statements. Three of the four, I deeply regret to say, are published on Sundays as well as week-days. They sometimes try to get clergymen to write serious articles for the Sundays; a wretched device, when the obvious tendency of the Sunday publication is to obliterate all traces of the sanctity of the day. To me personally the editors were very kind, and some of them would fain that I should contribute to their papers, but with this request I did not comply.

So far as I had an opportunity of mixing with the society of Los Angeles, I found it very kind and hearty. Several of our fellow-travellers in the Yosemité Valley were exceedingly hospitable. I could almost wish to record the names of three whose kind attentions exceeded all we could have looked for. Some of them boarded in the Lincoln Hotel, and our head-quarters being in the country they made us as welcome to its accommodation from time to time as if it had been their private house and we their oldest friends. I cannot help expressing special acknowledgments to the Caledonian Club and its excellent president, Mr. J. O. Maclean. We were always welcome there. Hardly had I arrived when Mr. Maclean arranged that I should meet the club, and, by way of "talk," give my lecture on the Life of Livingstone, which I did to a large and very interested audience. And when my worthy friend, the Rev. Dr. Ormiston of New York (a native of Lanarkshire) came to the city, a few weeks later, a grand reception was given to us both. Clergymen of all denominations and representative laymen sounded the praises of Scotland. And, of course, Dr. Ormiston and I were made out to be Scotsmen of the very highest order. I took it all *cum notâ*, discounting everything by about ninety-five per cent. But it was amusing (perhaps in a quiet way gratifying) to see what a wonderful people the Scots were held by the Americans to be. The amusing thing was that every one claimed to have some connection with the country. An Episcopal clergyman said he was proud to pay honour to Scotsmen, because the first bishop of the American Episcopal Church had been consecrated in Scotland, when they would not consecrate one in England. And at the end the hand-shaking was wonderful. "Let me shake hands with you, for my wife's grandmother was Scotch." "I'm from Nova Scotia, and my people came originally from Scotland." "I'm a *Mac*." "My name is Burns, and my boy is Robbie." It was very funny; but we were very happy. I wished that we were worthy of the half of it, for we did seem rather much of a mutual-admiration society.

At least, I could not help feeling next morning that more might have been said to stimulate the Scotch and all the Christian people of Los Angeles to new exertions on behalf of their Sabbath, which in that city, and in the community at large, needs greatly to be contended for. I have referred to the Sunday newspapers. There are Sunday theatres, Sunday saloons, Sunday excursion-trains, and Sunday picnics without number. While we were there a flaring advertisement appeared on the streets that for a succession of Sundays a certain aeronaut would ascend in his balloon at Santa Monica, a seaside place some sixteen or twenty miles off, and come down in his parachute. The railways ran trains to the place as quickly as they could provide them to carry the thousands that hurried to see the sight. What the effect must have been in dissipating serious impressions, if any of the spectators should have been at church in the morning, and stimulating vanity and frivolity, I need not say. Both in preaching and writing I took occasion to press the serious obligation on all the Christian people of the state to be on their guard against the lowering influences of what was the common custom, and to charge themselves with a sacred mission—that of testifying for God's truth and man's duty, and striving in every way to elevate the religious standard. One must remember that many of the Christian people have arrived but recently, that they are imperfectly acquainted with one another, and that they have been much occupied in building churches, and in other work needing and almost absorbing their immediate attention. The old Mexican spirit has not died out, and the usual disorder of new communities has not passed away, great though the improvement be on former days. There is still need of something like a solemn league and covenant to storm the intrenchments of the enemy and gain California to Christ.*

---

* I am tempted to introduce here part of a letter from H. M. Stanley to myself which I referred to at Los Angeles in my lecture on Livingstone, all the more effectively that Stanley is the connecting-link between America and Livingstone. When Stanley was in Edinburgh, after being at Berlin at the concocting of the Congo treaty, he told Dr. Livingstone's daughter (Mrs. A. L. Bruce) that he had read the "Personal Life" at Berlin, and that it had brought Livingstone so clearly before him that he felt new vigour in pleading for his plans. I had occasion to write to Mr. Stanley soon afterwards, and I asked him if he would be good enough to tell me whether he thought I had done justice to Livingstone. The following is from his reply:—"I read the 'Personal Life of Livingstone' on the Congo with very great pleasure, and as I closed the book I was convinced that it would be almost impossible to produce a more vivid or truthful picture of the good man than can be gathered by reading your book from beginning to end. There is no straining of the effect in it, but the Life reads smoothly as though writ by a master's hand. We see the poor factory boy at his ill-paid work grow into manly fulness; thence we follow him through a strange life's probation in wild lands and the troubled period of it, and the long, patient struggles of the heroic spirit to do its part well and bravely, until it is finally worn out, and the silver cord of life has snapped, and the well-merited eternal rest has been won. It is a poem, sir, of which you, the narrator of it, may well be proud of the privilege of having told it. Good-bye, and many thanks for your kind words to me.—Yours faithfully,

"HENRY M. STANLEY."

CHAPTER VII.

SOUTHERN CALIFORNIA AS A FIELD FOR EMIGRATION.

I THINK it may be useful and not uninteresting here to put down some facts on the suitableness of Southern California as a field for emigration. It is still true, as in the days of Martin Chuzzlewit, that very misleading statements are put forth by interested parties to induce the unwary to emigrate to colonial and other settlements, and many an honest man has been involved thereby in great loss and disappointment. I shall try to state things as they are.

People in Great Britain have very inadequate notions, for the most part, of the extent of the state of California. It is seldom apprehended that it is from seven to eight hundred miles in length, and from two to three hundred in breadth. When the discovery of gold was made some forty years ago in the northern part of the state, it was to that part of it chiefly that the rush of emigrants took place. It was San Francisco, in the north, that suddenly became a great and wealthy city. It was there, too, that the usual lawlessness of a mining population, dissevered from family life and from the influences of Christianity and civilization, showed itself, and gave a bad repute to Californian society. The notion got abroad that every second man in California carried a revolver in one hand and a bowie-knife in the other, and that no man who was not actually on fire with the gold-fever ought to commit himself to such dangerous fellowship. Even in the mining districts of Northern California, however, things are now much changed for the better. There is still a rowdy element, as there is in most of the new states of America; but it is confined to a limited class—the frequenters of saloons, the prize-ring, and the vile dens of sin—and respectable men who mind their own business, and lead a quiet and peaceable life, may enjoy throughout the state the same sense of security and tranquillity that is to be found in most other civilized parts of the globe.

About twenty years ago two things began to attract the attention of Americans to Southern California—its wonderful climate and its magnificent fruits. These two things are now doing for Southern California what its gold-mines did forty years ago for Northern. They are drawing to it a rapidly-increasing population, but in a much quieter way, and of a much more varied character than that which the gold-mines drew to the northern part of the state.

First, as to the climate, it is hardly possible to exaggerate its qualities. During the summer half of the year little or no rain falls, and you have an almost unbroken succession of bright, sunny days. The heat is considerable, especially in inland places—from 80° to 90° is not uncommon; but near the coast it is delightfully tempered by a refreshing breeze from the sea, and, unlike most tropical countries, the nights are comparatively cool. I found myself able to walk considerable distances in the middle of the day, not only without exhaustion, but with somewhat of the exhilaration that one feels in Switzerland. Work, too, can be done in the fields with a very high thermometer. Sunstroke is unknown, so is dog-madness. The soothing, balmy influence of this splendid spell of genial summer weather is felt by every one, and it makes life sensibly brighter and cheerier. One sometimes thinks with a chill shudder of the eastern winds and cold fogs that are not unknown even in summer in one's native land. Not that you require no precautions against cold; the changes of temperature, as the daily fogs fall and rise, are considerable, and have given rise to a saying that you catch cold in Los Angeles twice a day.

But it is winter which gives its best feature to the climate of California. Except when it is raining, winter is like summer. The nights are colder, but there is not much difference in the days. And this is the great attraction to the people of the eastern states and of Canada, many of whom are pouring into Southern California. They get tired of the severity of the eastern and northern winter. Once in California, they are loath to leave it. For consumptive people it is like the elixir of life. Every second person you meet tells you he came to Southern California for the health of some member of his family, and in almost every case the benefit was remarkable. With some precautions against the change of temperature between day and night, and with due arrangements for exercise in the fresh air and abstinence from exhausting toil, persons of weak chests and throats are enabled to live comfortably, and if the disease has not gone too far, they have every chance of recovery.

For fruit, Lower California seems destined to be the orchard of the world. Grapes, oranges, melons, apricots, peaches, plums, pomegranates, lemons, citrons, figs, walnuts, olives, and I know not what all besides, flourish amazingly. Of course, not all equally in every place. There are conditions of particular districts, to be learned only by experience, eminently favourable to some kinds, and perhaps unfavourable to others. But on the whole it is an unrivalled fruit region. If one kind of fruit be specified for which it is pre-eminent, it is the orange; and experience is now showing that a particular kind of orange, called the Washington navel, is the very best that grows. It is to be noticed, as modifying the garden character of the state, that Southern California presents a remarkable combination of mountain and valley. It is in the valleys that fruit is so flourishing. The soil, formed apparently in the bed of ancient lakes, is marvellously fertile. The rich vegetable mould extends in some places many feet—some say hundreds of feet—below the surface. Year after year crops are raised—not of fruit only, but of wheat, grass, and vegetables—without manure. If irrigation be applied, two crops of grain may be got in one season, and of alfalfa grass from three to eight. The soil is well adapted for farm produce as well as fruit. In the larger ranches (the old Spanish word is in constant use) cattle, sheep, and horses are reared, and ordinary farm produce is raised. It is more in the neighbourhood of towns that the culture of fruit prevails. The quantity of fruit produced is far greater than is required to supply the wants of the population. The less perishable kinds are transported far and wide. Every effort is made to convert what is perishable into durable forms by drying and by canning.

For some years back grapes have been so abundant that the wholesale price has hardly paid the cost of labour. A cent (halfpenny) a pound is considered a good wholesale price. An acre of vineyard usually produces from three to eight tons of grapes. But it is a troublesome crop to rear, and involves a great deal of labour. It is much more profitable to turn the grapes into raisins, but this requires a dry climate, at some distance from the sea, unaffected by the fogs. The orange is probably the most lucrative crop, on ground well adapted for it. But the orange does not bear well till about its eighth year, whereas vines have a fair crop in their third or fourth.

We have yet to mention the most outstanding peculiarity of Southern California, viewed as a field for farming, and especially for horticulture. We refer to the extraordinary distribution of water. Of rivers, streams, or surface running water of any kind, the supply is most limited. Great tracts exist where there is none. This is the more remarkable that the country presents great mountain ranges, which are among the most striking objects in the landscape. From the peculiarity of the soil, the water gets below the surface: sometimes it is within a few feet of it, and at other places you have to descend hundreds of feet before you come to it. If the water is near the surface, the trees and other plants send down their roots, sometimes to a great depth, and find the necessary supply of moisture. Many kinds of fruit trees do not require more water than they obtain in this way. The water percolates upward by capillary attraction, but does not evaporate from the top. In the driest weather the soil is moist a few inches under the surface. Vines do not need to be watered. The opinion has hitherto prevailed that oranges need an artificial supply; but this opinion seems to be undergoing a change. In many places crops of wheat and grass are also obtained without artificial irrigation. In some districts, and especially where more than one crop in the year is sought, artificial methods of irrigation are resorted to; and one of these, I regret to say, is the employment of town sewage water, which in hot weather is most dangerous, and in the neighbourhood of Los Angeles has given rise to several cases of typhoid fever. Artesian wells are not uncommon, and they yield a large supply. The American Government is at present devoting earnest attention to the best ways of dealing with "arid tracts," and trying to devise methods of bringing such water as is available to bear on the vast districts of desert that exist in some parts of the country. If the water difficulty could be successfully dealt with, Southern California would become more abundantly productive than perhaps any other part of the globe.

Now, "just here," as the Americans say, is the point where emigrants are most liable to be misled. I have before me a flaming advertisement respecting the land in a certain valley, which is offered at from eight to fifty dollars an acre. The land, it is said, has grown the premium wheat in the world; it has grown parsnips seven inches in diameter; it has grown eight crops of alfalfa in one year; it has grown two hundred and eighteen tons of sugar-beets to the acre; it has grown deciduous fruits of all kinds and vegetables of every variety in the greatest abundance and the finest bloom; and it is capable of growing cotton, tobacco, pea-nuts, and champagne and raisin grapes. The situation of the valley is high; it is free from fogs, and eminently favourable for health. Now, every word of this is probably true; but where the results specified were obtained, there must have been an exceptional supply of water—probably from an Artesian well. But Artesian wells are costly; the effort to get water by them may prove, after all, a failure; and irrigation by means of them is a laborious and clumsy process. The valley in question is well known to the present writer, and it is really a waterless plain. Men buying land there may fancy they are to grow rich; but after having spent their little all, they may be fain to leave it, go where they may. In general, we may say that those settlers in Southern California who have been fortunate in water arrangements have done well, and some who have had to wait may yet be aided by Government measures and enjoy final success. But in many cases the want of water has proved a fatal want, and it is well for settlers to find this out in time, and act upon it before they are penniless.

Before answering the question, What sort of emigrants should go to Southern California? it is necessary to bear in mind the effects of the "boom" of two or three years ago, and the influence it had on the price of land. During the boom, all manner of artificial means were taken to raise the value of land. Syndicates would buy up a large ranch, lay it out like a town in blocks and streets, build a large hotel, run a tram-line or a branch of a railway to it, and invite the world to buy it up in detail. Sometimes the scheme took, at other times it was a dead failure. But the effect of this was to run up the price of the best land everywhere to a very high figure; and, though it has fallen since that time, bargains in land are not easily to be had now. The expectation prevails that there will be another boom soon; but the wisest heads will do their best to prevent it acquiring the wild proportions of three years ago. The country is bound to prosper, for if there were nothing else to make it attractive, its wonderful properties as a health-resort will always bring to it a great influx of people. But in time the mining resources of the state will be developed; manufactories will be established to supply the people with many articles now brought from Chicago or St. Louis; the fruit industry will be placed on a more systematic and productive footing; possibly a considerable shipping trade will be established, especially if a project now talked of be carried out, to make San Diego the Pacific port for the large steamers that trade at present between China and San Francisco. No part of the world seems more sure of future increase and prosperity than Southern California.

Who, then, should emigrate to it? Certainly not all and sundry. I know of an impetuous, well-meaning Scotch lady who brought out a lot of women to the country so utterly unsuited for it that some ladies in California had to raise money to send them back. People with diseased chests need not come here, unless they bring with them the means of living for a winter or two; otherwise they will be unable to do justice to their ailments. Skilled mechanics will get splendid wages during a boom, but when the boom has "bursted," they may get no wages at all. Farmers who mean to grow grain and raise stock must purchase a ranch, which can now be got at a reasonable rate only in a somewhat out-of-the-way place, and if it has never been cultivated, can yield but little for a time. Probably the kind of thing that would suit the majority of emigrants best would be a small fruit-ranch of some ten or more acres in the vicinity of a town. Half of this might be an orchard; the other half would be a small poultry and dairy farm. It would be amply sufficient to maintain a horse, two cows, and a flock of poultry. A comfortable wooden house may be built for from £100 to £200. A well and windmill to raise water for domestic and ordinary farm purposes, with barn, etc., might cost other £80. The land (near town) might run from £20 to £100 an acre or more. There is always ready sale for eggs and butter. The conditions of life are easy: little fuel is needed, and little clothing; and the climate is so dry and warm that cattle hardly need any shelter, and buildings do not readily decay. A frugal proprietor might almost live on the produce of his dairy and poultry, and have the value of his fruit crop over and above. Service costs a great deal, and is difficult, almost impossible, to be had. Four or five pounds a month, with board, is the wages of a female servant; farm labourers have more. Settlers must be abundantly able to help themselves. In the great majority of farmhouses no servant is kept. There is but a very limited demand for clerks or professional men. Southern California is not the country for loafers or for shiftless fellows. Sharp men, who see what is needed, and can adapt themselves readily to the circumstances of a new country, are the men to get on. As in most other new countries, an emigrant ought not to be in haste to settle; if he can spend a little time in looking about him and studying the situation, so much the better.

The authorities make a most liberal allowance for education, and it is free to all. There is usually a full provision of churches in towns, and in country-places the church-going people generally attend the church of the denomination which happened to be first in the field. The settlers are commonly most neighbourly and obliging; and as to honesty, the risk of losing anything by stealing in rural districts is virtually *nil*. It hardly matters whether the house-door is locked at night. A settler may shut up his house, leave his live stock in charge of a neighbour, be absent for days, and have no anxiety all the time as to his finding everything on his return just as he left it, both inside and out.

It is said there are about ten thousand of her Majesty's former subjects settled in Southern California. Many of these are from Scotland, and more, perhaps, are Scottish Canadians. Most of them are fairly comfortable, many are rich, and all are high in praise of a climate which probably, if both summer and winter be taken into account, has no superior on the face of the earth.

CHAPTER VIII.

"*OUT AND ABOUT.*"

MY son's fruit ranch is situated about five miles from Los Angeles, in the neighbourhood of the village of Florence. Florence is but a straggling hamlet, and what there is save the glorious sky above it to entitle it to the name of the Tuscan capital it would be hard to say. There is no want of roads in these parts, for the whole country is laid out in rectangles, and usually at every half mile there are roads, broad and tree-lined, crossing each other at right angles. The quantity is ample, the quality—*une autre chose.* Near town the roads are properly built, but a few miles out they know nothing of road-metal, but consist simply of the native soil; and where there is much traffic, they are beaten and pounded in the drought of summer into sheer beds of dust. In winter, when the dust has become mud, the residents turn out and mend their ways by shovelling the mud from the sides on to the middle. At other times an effort will occasionally be made to contend with the dust by spreading straw over it, or eucalyptus leaves, or any other available rubbish. But really, when you consider all that the settlers have had to do, the wonder is that they have roads at all. I remember travelling some years ago on a stage-coach between Inversnaid and Loch Katrine in company with some Americans, who were in a boastful vein, and disposed to run down everything in Scotland. Compared with America, the lakes were small, the mountains low, the horses poor, the stage-coach paltry. "Well, gentlemen," I said, "you will admit we have better roads."—"Little thanks to you," was the reply; "you have had two thousand years to make them."

The country about Florence, as in many other places, is mostly laid out in vineyards and orchards. Some are large, covering hundreds of acres, but most of them are from five or ten acres upwards. The Nadeau vineyard, for example, is a large one. The first owner made money in the freight transportation or carrying business—conveying goods over the desert before the days of the railway—a rough and risky business in those days. Buying land cheap, he acquired a large quantity, of which his family now reap the benefit. The country is too flat and fertile to have much picturesque beauty, but the range of mountains in the horizon is always grand. The charm is in the climate. It is quite luxurious to find day after day the most glorious weather—a blue sky without a cloud, and in the evening that tender "after-glow" that seems to breathe the spirit of heaven. The vegetation is wonderfully rich. A very little labour and care will secure a most beautiful garden. Roses flowering all the year round, white lilies of incomparable purity, bushes of carnations with hundreds of flowers on each, marguerites with thousands, geraniums like trees, a hedge of blazing sunflowers twelve feet high, annuals in richest bloom, made our little cottage appear a corner of paradise. It was such a contrast to Edinburgh gardens, where all the labour you can expend is so little productive. The flowers seemed to say, Just stick us in the ground and give us a drop of water—it's all we ask.

I was favourably impressed with the people who own and cultivate the farms and orchards in the neighbourhood. Of course there were exceptions, but take them all in all they were respectable, serious, and neighbourly — people that would not see a neighbour in trouble without lending a helping hand. At Florence there is a little Methodist church, with a very worthy and earnest minister. When I preached, the whole neighbourhood seemed to turn out, and there was a happy family feeling pervading the assembly. At Vernon, in another direction, there is a Congregational church, the minister of it a devout, cultivated, and very agreeable man. Here I was even more at home. In these places people for the most part seem to be church-going, though there is a proportion of the careless and unbelieving. There are superior schools at both places. At Vernon, a new school was in the course of erection — a large and handsome building, that in our country would have cost from £1,500 to £2,000. It must always be said in honour of Americans that they do not starve their schools.

Shall we now make a little excursion of ten or twelve miles in the direction of the mountains, and become acquainted with Pasadena? It is a flourishing town, only seven years of age, with a population estimated at 14,000. There is not much of the appearance of town about it — only a street or two, the rest being suburbs, dotted all over with villas and cottages. It is more a winter than a summer residence; in fact, that huge hotel, the Raymond, dominating the town from a commanding height, shuts up its five hundred apartments in summer, and takes in guests in winter only. The winter climate is splendid for invalids. The hotel is named after a brotherhood that, like Cook and Son in England, organize excursions, and labour to make travelling easy. Pasadena is a choice spot, having many families in easy circumstances, whom the charm of its winter climate has induced to settle there. Like most other places, it has its proportion of Scotsmen. I met them in dozens in the very large and handsome Presbyterian church where I officiated. Sauntering along the principal street, I observed a store called "The Bon-Accord Emporium," or some such name. My heart gave a little leap at the word "Bon-Accord," the motto of my native city. I went up to the owner and said, "Mr. Brebner, are you not, like myself, from Aberdeen?"—"Yes," he said. "Did you know my father, an elder of the Free Church in Turriff?" I knew him more than forty years ago, having been then minister in a neighbouring parish; and in those days, just after the Disruption of the Church, every man who was so useful as Mr. Brebner was honoured by us all.

From one of our friends in Pasadena we got a little chapter of family history which shows vividly how some men get on. A relation of my friend's, with an ailment of the throat, had come with his wife from one of the middle states in search of health. Their means were small, and before they could make up their minds what to do, or where to settle, everything was spent. Thereupon, in order to get daily bread, the wife had to resort to teaching in Los Angeles, and by this means she kept the family alive. A friend sent him eighteen hundred dollars to invest; he became the borrower, and undertook to pay something like eighteen per cent. interest upon the loan. He bought seven acres at Pasadena, improving them with his own hand, and by-and-by selling at a considerable profit, which enabled him to repay the loan and buy other fifteen acres. These in like manner he improved, and was able to sell at a profit, and from this he went on till he has now very extensive property and ample means. But let no man reckon on repeating such an experiment. It succeeded simply because the gentleman came in the very nick of time. We hear much of successful cases of this sort; but many a man, just as laborious and persevering, has struggled and struggled and failed, because he lost the tide which bore the other to fortune. Success is blazoned abroad ; failure, though far more frequent, lurks concealed.

With another friend we made an interesting excursion among the mountains, having our picnic in a beautiful canyon in the Sierra. Our more immediate object was to call on a gentleman named Brown, son of the famous John Brown of Harper's Ferry, who lost his life in the cause of the slave, and has, most deservedly, been a hero with the negroes ever since. It was a difficult matter to get up the steep pass, for the roads were very rough and the day was very hot. And Mr. Brown's shanty was high up among the mountains—why so high it was hard to tell. Such as the road was it had been constructed with much hard manual labour by him and a brother recently dead, in whose memory a tombstone had just been erected on the crest of a neighbouring height. Unfortunately we did not find Mr. Brown at home, and we had to content ourselves with carrying off two magnificent stems of *Yucca gloriosa* from the mountain side. We regretted much that we had not seen him, for he is said personally to be a most interesting man, and he could have told us many things about his father. Near to his house, and built on land that once belonged to him, is a sanitarium, presided over by a lady-doctor. This lady we afterwards met in a railway-car a long way off. She told us much of the singularly unselfish and benevolent character of the two brothers, who seemed to lead such a recluse life. I cannot repeat what was not meant for the public, and might be distasteful to the man in whose praise it was uttered. But it surpassed the old story of the dying Sir Philip Sydney handing his cup of water to the common soldier beside him, with the remark, "Thy necessity is greater than mine." Poor though these Browns were, when they had any money it was wretched negroes and Mexicans that got the benefit of it. One seemed to understand better the character of the father—how he came to be such a friend to the slave, and how the slave had such an affection and veneration for him. And I remembered an anecdote of the Jubilee Singers which I had heard told by the late excellent and amiable Lord Ardmillan. In a drawing-room where the Jubilee Singers were giving a performance, he was struck with the heartiness with which they sang "John Brown." He went up to one of them and said, "You seem to have a great regard for John Brown."—"Yes," said the young man with emphasis; "and well we may. He *died* for us." And then, as if fearing that he had used too sacred an expression, fitted in its full reach only for another application, he added quietly, "But there was Another that died for us all."

One thing more before we leave Pasadena—it is a temperance town. I believe there is a part of it to which this remark does not apply, being under another regulation, but prohibition reigns in the original Pasadena. Not, I believe, by decree of the people, but as one of the conditions under which the city was originally established. It is not a place for testing prohibition, because, though the sale of drink is illegal within its borders, drink can be got so easily from neighbouring places. Still, there are no saloons in Pasadena. And as there are no saloons, there is no disorder or crime or open wretchedness. Nor does the reign of prohibition seem to have the least effect in driving away immigrants or retarding the prosperity of the place. Few communities have advanced so quickly or prospered so much. And it is far more likely that families will be drawn to settle there by the peace and prosperity which prevail in the absence of saloons, than that they will shake their heads and turn from it in horror because it affords no facility for the unwholesome excitements of alcohol.

Another trip in a different direction brings us to Ontario, in the San Bernardino valley, about forty miles in a south-eastern direction. We pass through Pomona, a rising and prosperous town, and find Ontario a much smaller community, but with some interesting features. It was "made" by two brothers from Canada—hence its name—who determined to spare nothing to turn it into a most attractive and enjoyable place of abode. Among other things which they did was to lay out a fine avenue, originally seven miles long, now nine. Four rows of trees line the avenue; in the centre of the trees there is a tram-car road, and on either side a carriage drive. It was intended that all along this avenue land should be sold in allotments, and thus a great community created. To a certain extent this has been done. I believe the brothers found their means unequal to the undertaking, and that the property has now passed into other hands. That it will ultimately succeed admits, we think, of little doubt; for the neighbourhood is very beautiful, and the dryness of the climate, free from the sea-fogs nearer the coast, is admirably adapted for fruit. The drying of grapes and other fruits can be carried on splendidly here. Another place in the neighbourhood, Riverside, has even finer capabilities for fruit.

But our chief reason for coming here was to visit a young friend, the son of an esteemed minister, who had recently bought land and settled in the neighbourhood of the railway station next after Ontario, Cucamonga. Readers may get some idea of how settlers from the old country get on from a description of this place. We had sent a card intimating our visit the day before; but letters have to wait there for their chance of delivery, and we were not expected. We walked from the station, and were happy to find our friend, along with a comrade who lived with him, at home. A wooden house, almost unfurnished, but with excellent capabilities, would have been quite comfortable but for the myriads of flies that covered the windows and buzzed about everywhere, and could by no means be got rid of. Our welcome was cordiality itself, the only regret being that it was dinner-time and there was no dinner. But being "right smart," and put to his wits, our host managed in a few minutes to provide for us abundantly and most creditably. Then a walk through the ranch to see the recently-planted vineyard. Our host's enthusiasm was delightful as he pointed out how well the plants had struck, and even of those that had not yet struck there was no cause to despair. "Hope springs eternal in the human breast," and every young ranchman looks out on a wonderful future. May it be realized and more! I have great confidence in the future of Ontario, and I think my friend's prospects are good; all the more that his principles are of the kind to guide him well.

In the afternoon we had a drive over the whole countryside. It is not a very difficult task to reclaim land in those parts, for in its natural condition it is not occupied by anything very difficult to remove. In fact, the chief enemy of the farmer there is the sunflower. It is beautiful to see the yellow blaze covering a great stretch of land—beautiful to all but the farmer, who finds that do what he may he cannot get quit of it. The ground is generally level, and if the rabbits could be shut out, and more water provided, the produce would be wonderful. All over this Ontario region we see fruit trees abounding and flourishing. Not only the vine and the orange, but the lemon, the olive, and many other species. Our drive embraced miles of the great avenue, till at last we reached the hotel. We left our friends after a very exhilarating day, glad to have got the opportunity of seeing settlers in the earliest stage of their undertaking, and thankful to find them in such good spirits notwithstanding the drawbacks of their wilderness life.

CHAPTER IX.

SEASIDE ON THE PACIFIC.

OUR first view of the Pacific was at the watering-place of Santa Monica, a few miles north-west of Los Angeles. It was, as usual, a charming day, and the deep blue of the ocean, stretching so far in every direction, was superb. That was the first sensation. When the eye and the mind had sufficiently drunk in the broad expanse of azure, the next feature to claim attention was the surf beating against the shore; and that, it seems, is a constant feature. The sea is never perfectly smooth at the edge. The Pacific does not deal in extremes; it is neither frightfully wild nor absolutely calm. Its genius is different from that of the Atlantic. The Atlantic can rave like a maniac or be as still as a sleeping babe. In the Pacific you have always the swell and surf to restrain undue familiarity; and bathers know this well, and have to accommodate themselves to it. And what they do is hardly worthy of a valiant people. Bathing consists mainly in playing with the surf, and there are few swimmers, as far as I saw, bold enough to get beyond it and enjoy themselves in the smooth, deep water. Perhaps this may be due to the practice of bathing in a sort of full dress, which admits of the ladies and gentlemen being together, and makes it hard for the gentlemen to break away to where few ladies could follow them.

Santa Monica is very prettily laid out, and is one of the places that have made wonderful progress in a few years. A Scotch gentleman told me that a few years ago he had been offered a piece of landed property for twenty-five thousand dollars. It did not suit him to become the purchaser, and a year or two ago it was sold for four hundred thousand. Among those who have lately come to settle at Santa Monica is a colony of ostriches. Not that they have come of their own free will; but an ostrich farm, that used to have its establishment at Los Angeles, is now removed to Santa Monica. The proprietor is an English gentleman, a member of a titled and ancient family. The time was when the farm was open to visitors on Sundays as well as other days; but a change came over the proprietor when Mr. Moody was at Los Angeles, and now it is shut on Sundays. To a man struggling for a living this is no ordinary piece of self-denial, and it contrasts strongly with the conduct of the aeronaut already referred to, who makes Sunday at Santa Monica his great harvest-day. Whether the rearing of ostriches can be made profitable is a question yet to be decided. The spot selected affords a natural protection from the sea-breeze, and the ostriches will not have to complain of want of attention. Yet every one deems it an odd experiment, and I do not think that the public entertain very sanguine expectations of its success.

Our stay at Santa Monica was but for a few hours; but to Long Beach, another seaside place farther south, we paid a visit of ten days. Long Beach is a very recent place, begun four years before our visit. For two years it advanced splendidly, but since the bursting of the "boom" it has been much quieter; and last year it had a great calamity. Its hotel, a fine, large building, built on the bluff that runs along the seaside, took fire, and was utterly destroyed. No attempt had been made to restore it; and having been the one hotel of the place, it is greatly missed. But there are numerous boarding-houses for the accommodation of the public. One of our party being rather feeble, my son brought his horses and buggy, that we might drive about. It may show the free-and-easy treatment to which horses are accustomed in California, that though there was a stable attached to the boarding-house, he thought it better to tie the horses to posts outside and lay down their hay beside them. Hay there is not like hay here; it is wheat cut green and allowed to dry, and seems to serve the purpose of hay and oats combined. There was a beautiful drive on the beach, eight miles long, with a surface as smooth as a table, and firm enough to bear the wheels without sinking. The fresh sea-breeze was always delightful and exhilarating; it was hardly possible for invalids to breathe it without becoming stronger.

The whole of Long Beach is on the property of one gentleman who owns an immense tract in the neighbourhood. Many years ago two brothers purchased two great Mexican ranches of many thousand acres, for which the price was only seventy-five cents an acre. I have no doubt that in the neighbourhood of Long Beach the land would now fetch hundreds of dollars per acre. The owners of these ranches, which still bear the Spanish names of Alamitos and Seritos, were kind enough to invite us to see their places. We went with the more pleasure that they were good specimens of the old Mexican ranch, and that the old adobé houses were still standing. The houses are more quaint than comfortable. The walls are of immense thickness, and the rooms of considerable size; but the Mexicans seem to have had peculiar ideas on the subject of windows. In their time the windows seem to have been mere holes near the top of the wall; these had to be lengthened towards the ground by the present owners. One of the ranches has a famous dairy, with a prodigious stock of cheese; and, oddly enough, the men in charge of it are Italians. The other is celebrated for its sheep. In "Ramona" there is a graphic description of what the sheep-shearing used to be in the old Mexican times, and of the marvellous expedition with which some of the Indians could perform the operation. They told me that the sheep-shearing was carried on in much the same manner still. I was reminded of what a beloved son, now no more, who had been at Buenos Ayres for health, used to tell us of the incredible celerity with which oxen were killed, flayed, and otherwise disposed of by the natives in the Liebig yards of that city. Nothing astonishes you more than to see great flocks of sheep grazing in apparent content on plains where all vegetation seems as much dried up as if it had been baked in an oven. But the sheep discover a little berry like a burr, the fruit of a very abundant plant, on which they can not only live, but thrive and fatten.

At Seritos there is a fine garden—at least, it used to be fine—and I could hardly forgive the proprietor for suffering it to fall into decay. The house, however, was old, and he wished to rear a better one in a different situation. In a country which has no real antiquities, these old ranch houses and gardens are the only places that go back beyond the existing generation. I should have thought the proprietors, who have profited so greatly by the rise of prices, would have been eager to keep them up precisely as they were in the olden time, with their spacious verandas, their vine-covered arcades and trellises, their magnificent trees, and all else that told of the earlier history. But antiquarianism does not pay.

While we were at Long Beach, the "Alliance Assembly" was holding its annual gathering there. The meetings last in all about a month. The prototype of this congress is the famous Chatauqua Assembly in the state of New York. The idea is to utilize the holiday season, in accordance with

American habits, for promoting the spiritual, intellectual, and social welfare and enjoyment of the people gathered at the seaside. The Long Beach Alliance Assembly is under the auspices of the Methodist Episcopal Church; but a catholic character is sought to be imparted to it by the invitation of ministers and members of other Churches to take part in it. There is a large tabernacle for the meetings; they begin at eight in the morning, and they go on till about ten at night. It may seem to our sober Scottish view rather a strange thing to combine prayer-meetings and class-meetings and revival-meetings with lectures on popular or scientific subjects, and with concerts, where Jubilee Singers do not exclude even their comic songs. Yet in the Life of the late Dr. Begg it will be seen that he highly approved of Saturday evening concerts, and we know that he was not the man to think badly of the play of humour. The idea is that man has a complex nature, and that if you honestly try to exercise and develop every part of it, even if you do so simultaneously, the effect is good. And my judgment is, that for people in holiday humour, sauntering by the seaside in the usual somewhat careless spirit of holiday-makers, the social effect is good; but that not much, if anything, is done for the positive advancement of religion. At the request of the superintendent, I gave my lecture one evening on the Life of Livingstone; and one forenoon I conducted a service for young men and women, speaking to them of the character of Christ. It is remarkable how large and steady the various attendances were. There was a meeting for children every morning at nine o'clock in the Presbyterian church, and the little building was always full. The Methodists always strive to kindle emotion, and herein are a great contrast to us. Methodist religion is pre-eminently a religion of feeling, with very little of doctrinal teaching. And I noticed—what pains one so often in America—a want of reverence. I heard painful instances at the Assembly of the evil habit of using Scripture language to point a jest.

One of the funny features of the gathering was the "camping out." You see a space allotted for "camping," and you find all manner of people dwelling happily in tents, with their horse and buggy at hand, the horse "hitched" to a tree, and never dreaming of the luxury of a stable. And then when it suits them the friends can have a nice drive along the beach, or wherever else they choose. If you like, we shall make a call at that tent in the corner, where an excellent Methodist minister, a friend of ours, resides. The minister's wife receives us, and conducts us over her "house." The floor is covered with a carpet, brought from the manse. In one corner is a sofa; that is the drawing-room. In another, a cooking-stove; that is the kitchen. In another, a table; that is the dining-room. In another, a shake-down; that is the bedroom. But the ground is so dry, and the air so fresh, and the warmth so genial, that it is nice and pleasant. The cooking-stove is seldom needed; and the fuel being wood, the fire is easily kindled and easily extinguished, without turning the tent into an oven.

And I must add this about Long Beach, that no liquor is sold in it. By appointment of its promoters, it is a teetotal town. I need not say that it is the most tranquil and orderly place you can conceive. Even with all the excursionists that the trains bring to it, such a thing as drunkenness is unknown. I never saw a policeman in it, nor found a police-office. People smile when you ask if there be such. What use would there be for them?

At Long Beach I was presented by an accomplished lady with a copy of a book which every one was reading—"Looking Backward." It was in its 130th thousand. A book with a very absurd plot, and, I am afraid I must add, an absurd drift. Its author is an able gentleman of Boston, a socialist; and its purpose is to picture a state of society in which socialism has triumphed, and is diffusing unnumbered blessings on every side. I read the book with great interest, because I am very desirous to obtain light from any quarter on social problems, but I must add with great disappointment. The plot turns on a supposed case of mesmeric sleep, passed through by a young gentleman of Boston, who fell asleep in 1887 and awoke all right in 2000! He looks round him on his native city, and finds it entirely transformed. An entirely new state of society has come to pass. There are no rich and poor, no drones that toil not neither do they spin, no private property, no grinding competition in business, no strikes or lock-outs, no greed, no selfishness, no money! Everything is the property of the State, and all labour, all business, all everything is managed by the State. And every one is easy, contented, blessed. Labour ends at the age of forty-five; after that you simply enjoy yourself. In place of money, you get a ticket which enables you to get all you want at the public stores, the store-keeper making a punch-mark in your ticket for what you get. And society has not reached this condition by a violent revolution; it has just peaceably slid into it, in accordance with the policy which is every day absorbing private and smaller enterprises and converting them into a few great concerns. It is almost incredible that a man in his senses should imagine that some of the strongest impulses of human nature would be quietly annihilated before a pleasing picture; that men would all of a sudden cease to struggle every one for himself, and devote himself heart and soul to the public good. Environments will do much, but will they ever eradicate the greed, the selfishness, the ambition of our nature? I grant that in "Looking Backward" there is much true benevolence and a fine sympathy with the children of labour; and the author does not plead for confiscation, nor write as one who would resort to violence. But the marvel is, to fancy that without violence this age of gold will come of itself! to ignore the great problem of human corruption, and take no account of the only means ever devised for solving that!

> " To think—I have a pattern on my nail,
> And I will carve the world new after it,
> And solve so these hard social questions—nay,
> Impossible social questions, since their roots
> Strike deep in Evil's own existence here,
> Which God permits."—*Aurora Leigh*.

As to socialism, I do not think many Americans proper have much tendency towards it; it is the foreigners that uphold it. And I agree with those who think that for a hundred years there will not be much serious trouble with socialism in the country, because there are so many outlets for the growing population. But when America is as densely peopled as Europe, with many more overcrowded cities and complaining, half-starved citizens, then will come the tug-of-war.

CHAPTER X.

SAN FRANCISCO.

HAVING completed our visit to the family of our son, we next proceeded by sea to San Francisco. We did not fancy the Mojavé desert again, especially as on the 1st August it would be much warmer than we found it on the 31st May, when it was quite warm enough. We embarked on board the *Santa Rosa* steamer at San Pedro, the port of Los Angeles. The steamer was most comfortable, but not the ocean. In the evening we stopped for a few hours at Santa Barbara, a delightful and thriving seaside town, and had a most pleasant little visit at the house of Mr. Alexander, whom we had known in former days at Toronto. Feeble health had brought him to the Pacific coast, and he was both benefited and charmed by Santa Barbara. Re-embarking at night, our next stoppage, on the following day, was at Port Harford, the seaport for San Luis Obispo, about a dozen miles inland. Here, too, we had friends, to whom also we paid a pleasant visit. San Luis is a thriving city, in the midst of a fine agricultural district. When we got back into the wide Pacific, we got far from a pacific reception. A nasty side swell was perpetually hitting our vessel and causing a most disagreeable motion. It gave us a miserable night, although we had no sickness; and we were in no ordinary degree relieved and gladdened when getting up in the morning we found ourselves entering the Golden Gate, and in a little set foot on *terra firma* on the wharf at San Francisco.

We drove to the Palace Hotel. It is one of the phenomena of San Francisco, and a comfortable house. It is one of the hotels where you may pay for your bedroom only, and take your meals at a restaurant connected with it, or wherever else you may please. The higher you go the cheaper your bedroom; and as you are always carried up in the elevator, height is a matter of little consequence. No doubt there is one article in high rooms which startles you a little—a coil of thick rope close to the window, to give you the chance of escape if the house should take fire! It is a gruesome thing to look at. I was assured, however, that the risk of fire was infinitesimally small, as the hotel is watched by night, and fire could not break out without being discovered in a very brief time.

A word on American elevators. The elevator is one of the characteristic features of American civilization. It is said that there are quite different types of elevator, as of character, in New York, Philadelphia, and Chicago. It is in the newest cities that the elevator prevails most, because all the hotels, banks, warehouses, and other buildings using it were erected after the elevator had come into general use. Chicago is said to have the fastest, its elevators running usually at the rate of four hundred feet a minute, and the quickest at five hundred! This is too fast even for some Americans themselves. In New York the number of elevators amounts to three thousand five hundred, in Chicago to four thousand. The highest of all elevators is that of the Washington Monument (which is five hundred feet high); but it goes very slowly, at the sober rate of one hundred feet a minute. In private houses the elevator is becoming common. It is not only an American article, as being used chiefly in that country, but the contriving and improving of all its parts and methods of work have been almost exclusively the work of Americans. The department of the patent office in Washington devoted to it is said to be quite a study. As a comparatively new city, San Francisco is great in elevators, and in many a big building the stair might almost be dispensed with.

The common sights of San Francisco have been so often described that I do not intend to repeat the operation. The bay is very fine; the Golden Gate a stately entrance; the rock covered with seals basking in the sun a rare curiosity; the public park a wonderful transformation of what a few years ago were sandy hills. Oakland, too, across the ferry, is an interesting place, an offshoot from San Francisco, but it seems to have hardly interfered with the rapidity of its growth. The city is conspicuous for its commercial architecture, many warehouses and hotels being themselves a study; otherwise its edifices are not very striking. San Francisco must always be interesting to us as the first great American city on the Pacific coast, the first great settlement of the Anglo-Saxon race in what is virtually a new country—Western America; the first spot, in what is destined to be a great empire, where the virtues and the vices of our civilization began to spread abroad.

We had the pleasure to make the acquaintance of Dr. Mackenzie, minister of the First Presbyterian Church, an active and most estimable pastor, enjoying the esteem of the whole community; and no one could have done more to make our stay agreeable and profitable. During our four days' stay in San Francisco, I preached in his church, and in that of Dr. Cornelius, formerly of Pasadena; I delivered a lecture on the Pan-Presbyterian Alliance in Calvary Church, and also in the church of my friend, Rev. Dr. Horton of Oakland; I addressed a ladies' missionary meeting;

and I performed the ceremony of marriage, the bride being an old servant of our own, and the bridegroom an excellent specimen of a Scotsman. But at the same time I contrived to see a good deal.

We naturally felt a great interest in the Chinese in San Francisco. The Chinese have already contrived to dispossess the barbarians. Just as the woody particles of a tree are supplanted by the stony material which fossilizes it, so the first town of San Francisco has been gradually transformed, and is now fully occupied by the Chinese. Ten blocks, forming the first San Francisco, where stood the first counting-houses, the first banks, the first town house, the first churches, have been transformed into Chinatown; they are occupied by some say forty thousand, others thirty thousand Chinese; no one else will dwell in them, and if the Chinese should finally be expelled, they would have to be rebuilt before any other race would settle in them. The Chinese question is one of the American difficulties. At first they were welcomed to America as much as any other foreign people; but the case is very different now. I remember some years ago hearing Dr. Talmage preach on the Chinese question in his Brooklyn tabernacle. He was indignant at the feeling that was getting up against them, and ridiculed the change that had come over the American people from the time when they invited them so cordially to come and help them to settle the west—" You dear Chinee, do come over and see us, *and bring your work with you.* We shall be so delighted to have you with us!" But now the Californian Government has passed a law forbidding them to come into their state, and the Supreme Court of the United States has declared the law competent. What is urged in favour of this course is that the Chinese will not amalgamate with the American nation as all other foreigners have done, and notably the Japanese. They come over without their wives, not to settle but to make money; they go back as soon as they have made their pile; they wear their own dress, even the pigtail, live and eat in their own fashion, speak their own tongue, worship their own idols, import all they use, food and dress, from China, and take no interest whatever in anything American. I think there is much force in all this; although it is true that had they been treated at first with more kindness and consideration, the case might have been different now.

Dr. Mackenzie kindly took me to see Chinatown. Accompanied by a guide, about eleven o'clock at night we visited some of the haunts of the Chinese: sauntered through characteristic streets, had a cup of tea (served with an egg) in a restaurant, peeped into some of their opium-smoking dens, saw them worshipping in their joss-house, and ended by a visit to their theatre. Late though the hour was, everything was in full play. The Chinese constitution seems to require little sleep; hence their ability for extraordinarily long hours of labour,—they are said to be able to work eleven days in the week. Chinatown, on the whole, is a miserable place, for the Chinese in America will spend hardly a cent they can help. They are a remarkably handy, industrious, and sober people, and make excellent servants, both in the house and in the field. But the absence of married women and of family life makes Chinatown very squalid and repulsive. What women there are are mostly slave-girls, owned by wretches who turn them to the vilest purposes, inhabiting certain alleys which at night are openly given over to vice. There is a good deal of mission work done among the Chinese, and with a fair amount of success; and the missionaries, male and female, speak of the Chinese as an interesting people. Those of them who are Christian are hated by their brethren, and are allowed as little intercourse as possible with them. We visited a Chinese school, but not a large one, and had specimens of their proficiency both in English and Chinese. The recent law, if it be strictly enforced, will soon reduce and finally extinguish the Chinese element; but it is probable that it will not be rigidly enforced, because no other labourers will be found to do the work of the Chinese. The wages of servants, as we have said before, all over California are very high; families that in our country would have two or three servants are compelled to content themselves with but one, and that one very often a Chinaman.

It is interesting to observe, in a new community, the provision for the interests of the higher education. In America universities originate in three ways—from Churches, from the State, and from wealthy individuals. A new university has just been projected by a wealthy Californian, likely, for extent of resources, to eclipse everything of the kind, not only in America, but throughout the world. The Honourable Leland Stanford, Governor and Senator for California, who through mines and railways has accumulated vast wealth, had an only son of the same name, who died lately at the age of eighteen or nineteen. "The Leland Stanford, Junior, University" is to be the monument of his parents to this youth. For its endowment lands have been set apart valued at fifteen million dollars. In addition, Mr. Stanford is now erecting buildings at Palo Alta, thirty miles from San Francisco, which are to cover sixty acres. I visited the place in company with Dr. Mackenzie, a friend of Governor Stanford, who himself usually resides at Washington. On the grounds of his country house, and in sight of the university to be, is a costly mausoleum, lined inwardly with Italian marble, the outer walls of the finest Maine granite, the resting-place of the ashes of the youth whose death occasioned the undertaking. Mr. Stanford's idea is to found an institution which will begin with a kindergarten, and end with the most advanced instruction that human teachers can supply. From first to last, the instruction is to be absolutely free. Boarding-houses will be erected for all the students, male and female, and a room will be given to each at the cost of a trifling sum to the caretaker. Board, too, will be supplied at prime cost. From careful inquiries made at one of the most fashionable hotels of New York, Mr. Stanford learned that the prime cost of the provisions there supplied was only two dollars and thirty cents per week for each guest; and it is expected that at the university the price of board will not exceed two dollars a week. Houses for the professors, library, laboratories, and every other appliance needed for the efficiency of a university will be most liberally supplied. The style of the university buildings is Moorish. Already several class-rooms have been built, one story in height; and it is expected that in about a year sufficient progress will have been made for beginning the work of teaching.

Mr. Stanford has not lost sight of the religious question in his undertaking. He does not believe in a system of education that overlooks the highest aspects and objects of life. He provides that in all its operations the university is to recognize two great principles of theism—that there is a God, and a future life. All that falls short of this must remain outside the Stanford University. I fear such a creed is too colourless to be of much avail. It is an odd thing to recognize God without recognizing his chief revelation of himself, and to bring in the life to come and shut out Him by whom life and immortality have been brought clearly to light.

Mr. Stanford is taking an active interest in all the details of his institution, and will leave no stone unturned to make it a success. His path is not free from difficulties, and no doubt he is finding that the question of the renowned Mr. Baird, "Will siller dae it?" has sometimes to be answered in the negative. It is said that he has great difficulty in finding a president.

The site is a very choice one—elevated, spacious, airy, with a sufficient amount of grown timber to take off the look of bareness that used to strike an Edinburgh eye in Donaldson's Hospital or Fettes College. A railway station will make the communication easy with San Francisco and other parts; and though no ground will be permanently alienated, facilities will be given for building dwelling-houses to accommodate parents or friends of the pupils. It is not easy to say what will be the result of this undertaking; probably some of us may think that the plan of combining every stage of education in the same institution, and confining young persons to the same spot from first to last, is somewhat artificial and of doubtful expediency.

While I was in California, and especially in San Francisco, I found considerable excitement prevailing in connection with excursion trips that had been organized to Alaska, the latest territory that has been acquired by the United States, purchased by them about twenty years ago from the Russian Government at a cost of seven million dollars. Every one who had gone this trip was enthusiastic over it, and whenever a stranger like myself fell into their hands, the most urgent representations were made that, at all cost, it should be undertaken. Alaska is the north-west corner of North America, and lies to the north-west of our Canadian dominions. It was acquired by the United States on the advice of Mr. W. H. Seward. Mr. Seward was ridiculed for his action in regard to what was said to be a mere collection of glaciers and icebergs; but its mines, its seals, its fishings, and its furs have already made it a most valuable acquisition. One is almost provoked at its passing into American hands. It ought beyond doubt to have belonged to Canada. Many a representation, I have been told, was made to this effect to our Government by our friends in British Columbia, who knew the value of Alaska, but in vain. The Government had no fancy for icebergs and glaciers. But now Alaska, apart from its strategic value, is becoming a centre of an important traffic; and as a most picturesque and interesting country is becoming to tourists in America much as Norway is to tourists in Europe.

One thing that I was told about Alaska I found hard to believe. I thought an experiment was being tried upon my credulity when I was assured that the territory of the United States extended farther west from San Francisco than the distance between it and New York on the east. But when I examined the map, and observed the longitude of the most westerly of a long string of islands included in Alaska, I found that what had been told me was literally true. After some hesitation, I decided, on considerations of time, not to go to Alaska. But I have heard much about it. At Long Beach, I met with a Presbyterian minister who had been for ten years a missionary to the natives—a race supposed to be of Japanese origin. The superstitions of the natives were very gross and very cruel, especially in connection with their belief in witches. But in that respect there is a manifest improvement. The United States Government neglected the place utterly for some years after acquiring it, and have only recently begun to attend to it. Its great attraction to tourists, besides the beauty of its shores and islands, is its glaciers and icebergs. The late Principal Forbes of St. Andrews would have enjoyed a rare treat had he known of them and seen them, for they seem to throw no little additional light on the formation and history of glaciers. The trip to and fro is usually performed in about three weeks. Steam-boats go on purpose, and the tourist is carried without trouble from place to place; but no doubt some would like more freedom. Visitors to the Pacific coast would do well to include this excursion in their plans. A more direct starting-point than San Francisco is Victoria, in British Columbia, and this is easily reached by the Canadian Pacific Railway.

I do not think I can bid farewell to San Francisco without saying a word about its cable-cars. For the most part, in other cities cable-cars have been limited to short and easy distances; but now in San Francisco they take the longest and the wildest flights. Yet, *a priori*, one would have said that San Francisco, with its steep and far-extended hills, was utterly unsuited for that form of movement. In the city itself another view has prevailed. The streets are now all alive with them, some running in one direction and some in another, often following each other at intervals of a minute or two minutes, and seldom more than five. Usually two cars are joined together, one open and the other closed—the open one like an Irish car, with low seats running lengthways, making it remarkably easy to get off or on. Till one gets used to the sight, it is like magic to see them bowling along in meek silence, with no visible motive force, this way and that way, backwards and forwards, stopping at the beck of any passenger, white, black, or yellow, and performing every motion with the ease and regularity of the solar system. The marvel is how one rope can stretch so far; how it can turn abrupt corners, climb high hills, scud along crowded streets—all apparently without hitch or accident. Yet so it is. And the result is going to be a great extension of San Francisco in the direction of its high hills. The enterprise of these Californians is a contrast to the slow caution of our people at home; as is also the emotion with which we have to witness the struggles of panting horses to the nonchalance and sense of ease that dominate the cable-car system.

CHAPTER XI.

NORTHWARDS TO BRITISH COLUMBIA.

FROM San Francisco you may reach the Atlantic coast either by the Northern Pacific Railroad, which is the more direct route, or by the Canadian Pacific, to reach the terminus of which, at Vancouver, you have a preliminary journey of eight hundred and ninety miles, through the northern part of California, the state of Oregon, and Washington Territory. For various reasons I preferred the latter route. The first part of the railway run has some glorious scenery. The Sierra Nevada on the east and the Coast Range on the west are running towards each other; the railway runs between them, skirting for a long stretch the banks of the river, passing through wooded ravines and rocky gorges and green meadows in endless succession; while in the background a chain of mountains as high as the Alps towers heavenward—Mount Shasta, the queen of the range, being about the same height as Mont Blanc, although to my eye far from as interesting or impressive. At one point the train obligingly stops to give you the opportunity of drinking a glass of soda-water from the soda-springs which you see bursting quite near out of the side of the hill, and rolling to the river in clear, cool streams.

The state of Oregon and Washington Territory are interesting, chiefly from their endless forests. Here certainly you must be about the head-quarters of the lumber world. The railroad has made these timber treasures of priceless value, and has placed the remark of the English commissionaire, that these territories were not worth a plack, on a level with that of the French general who ceded Canada to Britain, that he had given up only some acres of snow. But even to the rapid railway traveller these forests are apt to become a little monotonous, though single trees are often a study, from their vast magnitude and perfection of form; and the mountains are wildly picturesque. But very often the havoc of forest fires makes black and ugly gaps along the line, and the eye longs for a change. There is little cause for the most patriotic Briton regretting that these territories are not in the British Empire; for British Columbia is not less abundant in timber treasure, and for beauty of scenery it beats them all.

Forest fires are picturesque enough to see by night; the clear, bright blaze contrasts splendidly with the surrounding darkness, and it is pretty to see the nimble flame running up the tree so deftly, and leaping from branch to branch, as if it were possessed by the spirit of the squirrel. But they have their drawbacks too. The day may come when the vast amount of wasted timber will be grievously deplored, although as yet it is not missed. But the day has come when the smoke of these fires so clouds the atmosphere in the heat of summer that the beauty of the distant scenery is lost to the traveller. This was our unhappy experience. While quite able to appreciate the nearer beauty, all that lay beyond a mile or two was lost in the haze. We never had a glimpse of the far-famed Mount Baker or Mount Tacoma; for about a week we had to deplore the smoke. From Tacoma to Victoria we expected a sail of surpassing beauty through the wooded banks of Puget Sound: we seldom even saw the shore-line. Passing Seattle, the town recently reduced to ashes (as our insurance companies know too well), we expected a sensation in the sight of the new city rising from the ashes of the old: for anything we saw we might have passed it at midnight. As we drew near toward Victoria, on the third day of our journey, the atmosphere cleared considerably, and we could see the Union Jack waving a good way off. And pleasant though our three months' stay in the United States had been, and little though we had found to remind us of a foreign country, it was with a peculiar feeling of satisfaction that we stepped on British soil, and, though still six thousand miles from our fatherland, seemed to smell the freshness of our native air.

Victoria, the capital of British Columbia, is a beautiful and thriving little city, not on the mainland, but on the island of Vancouver. Till the Canadian Pacific Railway was opened in 1885, it was so remote and inaccessible as to have little or no vital connection either with the rest of Canada or the rest of the British Empire. This was indeed true of all British Columbia. Being on an island, Victoria is a few hours from the terminus of the railway, which is at the town of Vancouver, on the mainland. It enjoys a splendid harbour, the Esquimalt, and will soon, doubtless, command an immense traffic with Japan, China, and the whole east coast of Asia. This traffic has already begun. The route to Japan and China is shorter than from San Francisco, while the land journey from the east is also considerably less. The inexhaustible lumber stores of British Columbia, the mass of valuable minerals, the agricultural produce of the numerous districts which are adapted to farming, indicate plainly enough what its destiny must be.

Of all the places I had seen on the American continent, Victoria seemed the city where it would be most pleasant to live. The climate is charming, with hardly any winter; the sea comes rolling in among the wooded bays and headlands with a refreshing breeze which carries no bitterness in its blast, and answers to that sea-loving taste which seems natural to us islanders. The whole look-out is bright and lively.

Scotsmen have had a good share of the prosperity of Victoria. I am afraid that they have not kept themselves in all cases unspotted by the vices to which a new place is subject, far off from civilizing and Christianizing influences. Being so much cut off from the Old World, Victoria, in its early days, followed in the wake of the cities of the American Pacific in certain habits which have not been for its good. Of recent years there has been a moral advance which is very gratifying, and encourages the hope that it will have a bright future in all that makes for the prosperity of a community.

There are two other towns in this part of British Columbia, close to the western terminus of the Canadian Pacific, that deserve a passing notice. New Westminster, on the Fraser River, besides its great sawmills, enjoys a pre-eminence as the centre of the salmon canning business. Apropos of sawmills, I ought to say something of the marvellous timber produce of these regions. It is not merely the abundance but the excellent quality of the timber that is so marvellous. A gentleman told me that near Seattle he had seen a plank, to be made use of in the palace at Honolulu, upwards of a hundred feet long, that was in its entire length absolutely without flaw. A single sawmill in that region cuts up three hundred thousand cubic feet a day. If ever nature formed ground for trees, it is in these regions of the west. As for the salmon, I hardly expect that the statements I am to make will be believed. I did not do what a fellow-traveller did—put down certain facts in a note-book, and get two fellow-travellers to sign an affidavit that they were correct. On the wharf of a cannery at New Westminster I saw salmon piled much as herring are piled at home after a good night's fishing, and I was told that twelve thousand had been caught that day. In the cannery itself fifty thousand cans are filled daily by a large staff of workers, some Canadian, some Indian, but chiefly Chinese. I did not feel that my love for canned salmon was greatly stimulated by the sight of the process. I was told that the owner of the cannery would probably net £20,000 as this year's profit. But the most remarkable fact I have to mention is that, as we passed along the banks of the Fraser River by the Canadian Pacific Railway, we saw the water literally black with salmon for about a hundred miles. It is their habit, in going up the river, to keep near its edge; and whenever a piece of rock projects from the bank and makes broken water, the salmon, instead of going round it, go right through the foam with a leap and a splash, while a shoal are gathered in the rear waiting their turn. At other places you see shoals moving slowly upward. The quality of the fish at this season is not very good. What we got at the hotels was generally of very inferior flavour to the salmon at home. I am told, however, that earlier in the season the flavour is excellent. It is said, too, that such as they are in summer, they are better adapted for canning than the other fish.

Vancouver is the youngest city of the three. Its site was unmitigated forest in 1885, and in June 1886 every building that had been erected was burned to the ground. The city is literally only three years old. And much though I have been used to the sight of cities of rapid growth, I must say that Vancouver beats them all. It is already a city of long streets, big blocks, handsome churches, and elegant villas. The Vancouver Hotel, built by the Canadian Pacific Railway, is as commodious and handsome a house as you could desire. Many persons connected with that railway have bought lots and built blocks in Vancouver, of course with the object of "booming" the place. And now the price of land is simply ridiculous. I was told of a couple of building stances that had been sold lately for thirty-two thousand dollars. Whether this boom will last is doubtful; but the town seems to grow apace meanwhile. More than one church is in its second edition, the first having proved too small. It is difficult to tell the present population of Vancouver—probably twelve thousand. It is not any special industry, but the fact of its being the terminus of the railway, that has given birth to it. It seems to me that this interesting young city will be moulded more according to the wholesome pattern of the Canadian cities than the more excited and feverish example of San Francisco. Its zeal for churches is very remarkable. Besides the Presbyterian, there are Methodist, Independent, Episcopal, Baptist, and Roman Catholic churches in it; and it will not be behind other places in the quality of its schools.

In all these three cities I was able to do a little service. The minister of the Reformed Central Presbyterian Church in Victoria, Rev. P. M. Macleod, was an old student and personal friend. I preached in his church, and likewise in that of the Rev. Mr. Fraser; and in Victoria, New Westminster, and Vancouver respectively I gave a lecture on the Pan-Presbyterian Alliance. I am happy to say that this lecture was well attended and well received in all these places, the more especially that I sought to divest it of all sectarian tendency, and to direct it not merely to making the audience better Presbyterians but better men. The people had much to learn both of the history of Presbyterianism since the Reformation and of the extent and diffusion of the Presbyterian Church. I always tried to impress on them that we lay under great responsibilities in being members of the Presbyterian confederation—members of a Church of such extent, and that had no cause to be ashamed of its history, no cause to be ashamed of its martyrs, no cause to be ashamed of its leading ministers and missionaries and laymen; and that we ought all to feel impelled by this consideration to walk worthy of our brotherhood and our ancestry, and strive to emulate them in self-denying efforts to advance the glory of God and the welfare of men. In most cases, ministers of other denominations were present, and thanked me cordially at the end. In one case, the Prime Minister of the Province, a zealous Presbyterian, moved a vote of thanks. All the Presbyterian ministers I met seemed to be active and earnest men: three out of five had got, or were getting, new churches built; and their flocks appeared to be in sympathy with their spirit.

Before bidding a final adieu to the Pacific coast, I must emphasize what I have hinted at before as to the great importance which this region seems certain to attain in the not very distant future. It is hardly to be questioned that in a few generations hereafter the shores of the Pacific—both American and Canadian—will be as densely peopled as the shores of the Atlantic have been, and will be the homes of peoples not less prosperous, not less intelligent, not less important as factors in the history of the world. This belief rests on obvious considerations. Nature has been far more bountiful on the western seaboard. These mountains are full of treasures of which but a fraction has yet come to light. In British Columbia, Washington Territory, and Oregon, you have forests of the finest timber, so inexhaustible that though enormous tracts have been destroyed by forest fires, the loss hitherto has not been so much as felt. Throughout these regions you have many tracts remarkably adapted for agriculture. The Pacific coast—especially the Canadian part of it—has admirable harbours. The fishing-grounds, as we have seen, are unrivalled. Southern California is unsurpassed for its climate and its fruits. On many of these parts the chill fingers of frost are seldom or never laid—the rigours of winter are unknown. A lady in Victoria informed me that her maid-servant (who had been brought up near the moors of Carnwath) asked her, somewhere about the month of February or March, at what season of the year it was winter there, as it had been nothing but summer since she came! Regions like these must have a remarkable future. The only unfavourable consideration is, that the very luxuriance of nature and the very sweetness of the climate may enervate the inhabitants, and keep down the spirit of enterprise and perseverance that bleaker climates and more barren soils have had not a little to do in stimulating.

Then the question presses itself on one, What will be the moral and religious future of this region? Now, if the beginning were to be held necessarily to represent the future, there would not be much to encourage one in dealing with this question. The beginning of Northern California was the gold discovery, with all its habits of rowdyism, ungodliness, and immorality. We have seen how unworthily the Sabbath is kept in Southern California. And British Columbia likewise had a poor beginning. It was long before any provision was made for religious ordinances. I regret to say that some Scotsmen in these parts became notorious above others for habits the very opposite of those in which they were trained at home. Sabbath-breaking, drinking, and licentiousness were often found linked together, like a threefold cord not easily broken.

But on the other hand one is encouraged at the testimony one hears on every side that *a great improvement has taken place in recent years.* Whatever may be the state of San Francisco to-day, it is not as it was in earlier years, when a murder a day indicated the temperature of crime. If there was little salt in the early community, a good deal has been imported in recent years. This is the hope of the Pacific coast. The emigration of recent years has poured into New America hosts of the best Christian families from the eastern states, from the east of Canada, and from other countries. A new leaven has come in to leaven the lump. Already in many instances the change has become quite apparent. Except in saloons and other dens of sensuality, life and property are as secure in these parts as in the most orderly regions at home. Churches abound; and though there are too many instances of ministers coming there who have been failures or worse at home, there are many of them full of earnestness and activity. When Mr. Moody was in these parts his meetings were thronged by eager multitudes, and a great impression was made. Such of the week-day prayer-meetings as I attended had, in proportion to the congregations, a much larger percentage present than at home. All this gives encouragement; and yet one has the feeling that unless a more aggressive and powerful combination of forces is brought to bear on the citadels of evil, their power will not be broken.

What, then, is the prospect of such a combination? The zeal for ordinary church arrangements has been great, but I confess I did not find the clergy and other earnest Christian people I met with in a very aggressive mood. But one must remember two things. In the first place, there has been an immense amount of effort employed recently in church-building, in paying up debt, and other necessary arrangements for Church work in a new community. And in the second place, every second minister and every second inhabitant has but come the other day. This is especially true of cities like Los Angeles that have sprung up like Jonah's gourd. Most of the people are new-comers, and total strangers to the rest. Few ministers have been there more than five or six years. It is rare to find a settler of twelve years' standing. In Los Angeles, after preaching to some seven or eight hundred people, I asked the minister whether one in twenty would be a native of the state. Not one in fifty, was the reply. This makes all slow to accept responsibility, or to look all round and devise measures for the good of the whole community. I cherish the hope that in a few years there will be more mutual acquaintance, more mutual confidence, and more sense of responsibility. On one point there is special need of concentrated attention—the state of the Sabbath. Unfortunately, unlike the other states, California has no Sabbath law. Nor will it be easy to secure such a law. In Oakland, which is to San Francisco what Birkenhead is to Liverpool, a meeting was lately held on the subject of a Sabbath law. When the meeting divided, one hundred and five were against any such thing, and only ninety-six in favour. The hundred and five included several members of a sect called "Seventh-day Adventists," who believe in the second advent and in the seventh day of the week as the true Sabbath. There are many Jews in San Francisco who are against the *Christian* Sabbath. There are many Germans who are practically the same. There are many Irish Catholics who despatch religion in the morning, and care not what they do after that. There are many nominal and indifferent Protestants. The true lovers of the Sabbath are but a fraction of the population. I have been urging on the ministers that even where success is for the present hopeless, they ought to try to keep alive the consciences of their people on the sanctity of the Sabbath. And I had a striking proof of the benefit of this from a brother who, soon after being settled, found a Sunday trip advertised by a company of which some of his own people were leading members. He forthwith preached on the claims of the Sabbath, and though he did not defeat the trip, he killed it, very few having gone, and he made it impossible that such a thing should be proposed again.

Two things, I think, must be apparent from this sketch — the vast importance of the whole Pacific coast, and the difficulties that exist in thoroughly Christianizing it. I hope our people at home will think of these things, and as they sing and pray, "Jesus shall reign where'er the sun," will bear in mind the sunny shores of the Pacific.

CHAPTER XII.

THE GREAT CANADIAN HIGHLANDS.

FROM Vancouver we took places in the Canadian Pacific, leaving at noon on a Friday, with the purpose of reaching Banff about midnight on Saturday, and of spending the Sunday there, the most attractive spot in the Canadian Rockies. We had not gone far when we were struck with wonder at the marvels of the railway. It is not possible to conceive a tract of country less adapted for such a road. Along the banks of the Fraser River, and far beyond, it is carried over the wildest and roughest country you can conceive. It is one continuous series of excavations along the sides of mountains, of high trestle bridges over ravines and chasms, tunnels through projecting shoulders of rock, with hardly a chance of any of nature's levels. And this really goes on for more than six hundred miles, until the prairie is reached, east of the Rockies. The succession of beauty and interest is endless, and the wooded mountains are magnificent. One does not know the grandeur of the British Empire until one has been whirled in the railway across British Columbia. Without disparagement of our Scottish mountainous regions, they must yield the palm to these magnificent stretches of highland scenery. You do not ascend any point as high as Sheppard's Pass in the Colorado Rockies, of which I have spoken, although you have to "loop" the line at one point and get to the watershed by the "circumbendibus" process. The greater part of the six hundred miles is almost without inhabitants, with the exception of those whom the railway itself has brought. And the railway villages are generally very rude and primitive. I believe that to tourists and sportsmen the country is exceedingly attractive, and doubtless it will fill up in many ways as time rolls on.

Glacier Point is a most interesting spot, about five hundred miles east of Vancouver. I wished much to spend a day here, but could not have done so without trespassing on the Sabbath rest. Extraordinary exaggerations have been circulated about the glacier, which some would make out to be larger than all the Swiss glaciers put together. This is out of the question, but all accounts testify that it is one of extraordinary magnitude and interest. I heard a great deal of it from fellow-travellers, but need not produce their accounts at second-hand. A few stages beyond Glacier Point is Banff, often called Banff Springs and Banff National Park. This is worthy of an ampler description.

Banff is situated very near the eastern edge of the Rocky Mountains, and was named after the little county town at the mouth of the Deveron through the influence of Sir George Steven, one of the railway magnates, who was a native of the place, or at least of the county. We cannot grudge this distinction to Banff; but if the character of the scenery had determined the name, Braemar would have been more appropriate. Its situation is superb. The Bow River, passing through the Rockies, affords to the railway a means of penetrating the mountains at about 4,500 feet above the sea-level. The domain which has been constituted a National Park for Canada is upwards of twenty miles in one direction and ten in another; but the Canadian Pacific Hotel may be taken as the centre of the Park, and the view from it is superb. The Bow enlivens and beautifies the wooded strath, from which ranges of mountains rise to great heights on either side. But, indeed, on all sides there is quite an amphitheatre of mountains, some clothed with pine almost to their tops, but most of them conspicuous for their masses of bare rock, suggesting the origin of the name "Rockies." When we reached Banff we were afraid that the haze which had shut out so many fine mountains from our view was to play us the like trick again. But a heavy rain had fallen between Saturday and Sunday, and when we came out of the little church on Sunday—where, by the way, we heard a most excellent sermon—the whole sky had cleared wonderfully, and the sun, shining in all his strength, poured his glory on the wonderful panorama that stretched on all sides around us. And this weather continued till we left the Rockies, and in a great degree reconciled us to the loss of the "Selkirks" and of other ranges that ought to have been seen, some of them in the glitter of their perpetual snow.

Undoubtedly, Banff is a place of unrivalled capabilities, and in days to come will be looked on with delight by many a Canadian and other eye. The Sulphur Springs which gush from the rock near it are said to be a powerful remedy for rheumatism; but it is the lovers of wild, lovely, picturesque nature that will form its great constituency. The Dominion Government is liberally disposed towards it, but even the handsome grant of 25,000 dollars at a time cannot do much in the way of constructing mountain roads and otherwise opening up the glories of the scenery. We look forward to a time when the whole Park will be intersected with beautiful drives, and the place visited by hundreds of thousands. Already one pretty drive of ten or twelve miles has been opened to Miniwonga, "the lake of the evil spirit," roughly rendered in common parlance "the devil's lake." It is said to be a fine lake for fishing. This year the medical men of Canada chose Banff for their annual congress. Between one and two hundred attended, just about the time of our visit. We met many of them, all very kind and pleasant, and we heard no difference of opinion as to the unrivalled beauty and interest of the place.

As we arrived only at midnight on Saturday, there was no time for the minister to discover me, and for once I had the privilege of hearing a sermon. The entire service was very admirable—devotional exercises, sermon, and delivery being nearly all that one could desire. Mr. Macleod is a young man, but seems admirably fitted for the place. The stated membership of the congregation is but fifteen; the rest come from the hotels. I should have thought his situation rather trying, especially as there was no manse, and he and the schoolmaster lived together in very plain lodgings. But I was delighted to find the minister in excellent spirits. As a Canadian student he had been accustomed to a pioneer ministry, and now he felt quite at home. His presbytery extends from east to west five hundred miles, and in the other direction its limit is the North Pole!

The secret of his happiness is his public spirit, his interest in his work, and readiness for every feasible undertaking. Besides Banff, he had other stations to supply. The nearest of these was fifteen miles off. He usually had evening service there, and the only way of reaching it was by walking along the railway track. Another station was seventy miles away. At one time he had to supply a vacant charge more than a hundred miles distant; but Canadian energy thinks nothing of a hundred miles.

This young congregation showed a catholicity of spirit not always to be found. There are some Episcopalians at Banff who as yet have no church. The Methodist congregation accommodates them in the morning and the Presbyterian in the evening. Where can the mother country produce such an instance of the brotherly spirit?

CHAPTER XIII.

THE NORTH-WEST, MANITOBA, AND TORONTO.

AFTER we left Banff (at midnight), and emerged from the Rocky Mountains, we found ourselves at daybreak on the vast prairie that stretches across the North-West Territories and the province of Manitoba on to Winnipeg. The first part of the prairie is rather desolate. The soil is thin, and at some places so impregnated with alkali that in the distance you would suppose you saw a lake of milk or a meadow of snow. It is here that one might have expected to see the buffalo, of which there were myriads a few years ago. But the buffalo is rapidly approaching to the condition of an extinct animal. There were plenty of bleached buffalo bones gathered in heaps by the Indians to be used by the sugar-refiners, and at some stations there were sets of buffalo horns for sale by Indians, who seemed to be doing a very good business in the article; but of live animals we saw none. The farms at first are few and far between, although I believe that much of these North-West Territories (Alberta, Athanaska, Assiniboia, and Saskatchewan) is admirably adapted for agriculture. After a day and night of hard travelling, we were in Manitoba. This is the vast agricultural region which is believed to be capable of supporting millions. The outlook was different now. Neat farm-houses, well-tilled farms, churches, and towns indicated a region much further advanced. The great drawback is the severity of the winter; but many people say that they get used to the cold, and that many places are colder.

Our destination was Winnipeg, the capital of Manitoba. It is a city of between twenty and thirty thousand inhabitants, very recently begun, but a most thriving and attractive place. The unusual width of its streets—one hundred and twenty feet, if I remember right—gives them a spacious and distinguished appearance. A few years ago Winnipeg was the scene of one of those gambling "booms" which are sure to be followed by a great reaction. Capitalists at a distance ran up the price of land to a ridiculous figure, and when the illusion was scattered many were ruined. Crowds came to Winnipeg only to be disappointed, and were obliged to leave it, go where they might. The city now seems to have recovered from the effects of that movement, and is advancing at a sure and steady pace. I was delighted to see the orderliness of Winnipeg, and especially its high standard of church-going and Sabbath observance.

I preached (as usual) in two of the churches—St. Andrew's and Knox's. In both I had congregations of from one thousand to twelve hundred; and I understand that this was not much in excess of the usual.

Manitoba College, founded by the Presbyterians almost as soon as Winnipeg itself, is the most considerable institution for advanced instruction in the province. Along with an Episcopal, a Roman Catholic, and now (I believe) a Methodist college, it forms the University of Manitoba, and has contributed more graduates than all the others put together.

In Manitoba a great struggle has just begun for another object. When "confederation" took place, it became legal for the Roman Catholics to have separate schools supported by rates, and it also became legal to make use of the French language in these schools. Against this arrangement a strong resistance has arisen, as being likely to perpetuate a condition of things which in Quebec has been very disastrous. I have a strong conviction that that resistance will prevail, and that the unfair advantages to Roman Catholics and the unpatriotic use of the French language, which in a province like Manitoba are entirely out of the question, will soon cease and determine.

Hospitality in Winnipeg took the form of carriage drives. Our landlord of the Clarendon Hotel, Mr. Bennett, an enthusiastic Scotsman, took us to the gate of Fort Garry, the only remains of the station of the Hudson Bay Company before Winnipeg was built, and to the suburb of St. Boniface, where the Roman Catholic colony of French Canadians have their schools and other establishments. Professor Bryce took us to Kildonan, the old Sutherlandshire settlement, peopled by Highlanders about the beginning of the century, under the auspices of the Earl of Selkirk ; and the Rev. Mr. Hogg took us to Sir Donald Smith's, where there is a small herd of living buffaloes that, in the absence of the wild animal, every traveller likes to see. There was an entertainment going on in the city of a peculiar kind. A hall, beautifully decorated with flowers and evergreens, was given over for each evening of the week to one or other of the congregations of the city, who undertook to provide songs, recitations, piano and other performances, for the enjoyment of the audience. On the night when we were there the great sensation was a Japanese marriage. Some thirty young men and young ladies of the church were dressed in Japanese dresses, and went through the ceremony with great correctness. The presents to the bride were not very costly, generally toys, but every person brought something. The object was to provide funds for a children's home, and if all the meetings were as crowded as the one we attended, the success must have been great.

In the North-West Territories and in Manitoba the law of prohibition prevails. I understand that this arrangement was adopted first with a view to the Indians, who would have ruined themselves, body and soul, if they had had free access to liquor. The law, I believe, has had an excellent effect on the whole, especially in new mining communities, where the temptation to drunkenness is usually so great. There seem to be some exceptions, however, to its enforcement. The Canadian Pacific Hotel at Banff, for example, has a license, obtained through the influence of the railway company, to which it belongs. What precisely is the law in Winnipeg I am not quite sure. I have heard that the Lieutenant-Governor of Manitoba has power to confer licenses in exceptional cases. Certainly there are very few saloons in the city. I was told that if a license were asked for a particular place, and five out of the twenty nearest inhabitants objected, the license was refused. This gives rise to some murmuring against the power conferred on minorities; but it keeps down the number of licenses, and it contributes to the peace, the good order, and the prosperity of the city.

It is a long cry from Winnipeg to Toronto. First a land journey of more than twenty-four hours through a rich and interesting region to Port Arthur, then a day's sail through Lake Superior, another through Lake Huron, and four hours of land journey to Toronto. The lake scenery was sometimes beautiful, especially that of Lake Huron; and the passage through the canal that connects the two lakes, with the setting sun illuminating the two villages—the American Sault Ste. Marie on the one side, and the Canadian Sault Ste. Marie on the other—was exquisite. Provincially "Sault" is pronounced Soo, and the passage is always spoken of as going through the Soo.

One experience of an unusual kind may be noted. In the middle of the night, in the first part of the journey, we came to a trestle bridge which had in some degree subsided. The authorities knew of it, but not the passengers. To those of us who were struggling hard to woo sleep, it was hard to be constantly conscious of something impeding our progress— going forward a little bit and back a little bit, as if our engine were disabled and could not drag its load. The explanation we got in the morning was that the carriages had been detached from the engine, which had been placed behind and had pushed them on to the edge of the bridge. Then a wire rope had been attached to the carriages and fastened to an engine on the other side of the bridge, which slowly drew them over. Two or three hours were consumed in this operation, but we had cause to think ourselves fortunate in comparison of some previous passengers who had had to walk over, and others who had been detained for many hours. The Canadian Pacific Railway crosses hundreds of trestle bridges; and I have counted as many as ten stories of trestles, one above the other. Every bridge is watched and examined daily, which makes travelling over them comparatively safe. If an unobserved subsidence should take place the consequences might be awful.

As you draw near to the capital of Ontario you get a better idea of the productiveness and comfortableness of the province. The farms and farm-houses are very attractive, as if they were all the abodes of peace and plenty, as many of them no doubt are. I will not linger over the city of Toronto, nor speak of its marvellous progress since I last visited it nine years ago. But this I will say, after visiting many American cities, and especially those of the Pacific coast, that Toronto is very different from most of these. No streetcar runs on the Lord's day through its streets. No saloon is open for drinking. No newspaper is published on the first day of the week. No theatre or place of amusement is open. Toronto is a very Scotch city, and Ontario is a very Scotch province; and among the points in which this feature is most apparent is the tone of Sabbath observance.

I had expected to pass through Toronto unobserved, but I found that where the carcass is thither the eagles are gathered together. The eagles were ministers desiring pulpit help; so I preached in two churches, in both cases to large and imposing audiences. The newspapers were more than usually eager to make out that far-off fowls have fair feathers, and at my hotel I had no fewer than three visits from editors wishing for my manuscripts and anything else they could fish out of me.

I was extremely gratified at the many proofs of the progress of the Presbyterian Church in Canada, and its great activity. It has paid especial attention to the North-West, and is undoubtedly the leading Church in those parts. Wherever I was I made inquiry as to how the union of the three Churches was working. Generally I got a very gratifying answer. All were practically one, and it was almost forgotten with which section ministers had been previously connected. Some were not so sure about this; but it is beyond doubt that the Church has made extraordinary progress since the union.

It happened that the American Association for the Advancement of Science were holding their annual congress at Toronto, and we were in time to hear a little of their wisdom. We were naturally attracted to a lecture on Niagara by a Washington professor. I am afraid I must say that he contrived to make a grand subject dry and uninteresting. He brought out one important fact, however—that since reliable observations began to be taken, the cataract had receded at the rate of from four to six feet per annum. This is about a mile in a thousand years. The cataract seems to have receded in all about seven miles, but there is no certainty that it has done so at a uniform rate. We were delighted in calling on an old Edinburgh friend, the Principal of the University, to greet him as Sir Andrew Wilson, and to shake hands in his house with his brother Principal of Montreal, Sir William Dawson; and to find them occupying places of honour in the association, and enjoying in a high degree the esteem of their brother *savants* of America.

A question that is absorbing an extraordinary amount of interest in Canada at the present day is connected with what is called the Jesuits' Bill. There is an excellent statement of the whole case in the October number of *Macmillan's Magazine* by Professor Goldwin Smith. Two years ago the Society of the Jesuits got itself incorporated, with the right of a corporation to hold property, and then they instituted a claim to property in Quebec amounting to two million dollars, which, it was said, had once belonged to them. The Quebec authorities, after a correspondence with the Pope, in which the Pope was allowed to determine to what parties the money should be given, passed a measure—avowedly a compromise—giving them four hundred thousand dollars. Then it came before the Dominion Government to determine whether this was competent, and with the exception of thirteen members they voted that it was. The Governor-General, and also the Crown authorities in England, have both successively upheld this decision. But it is very generally felt that if technically competent, the act of the Quebec legislature was morally wrong, and that it was most humiliating to let the Pope have his finger in the pie. A powerful association has been formed, called the Equal Rights Association, to protest against unfair advantages being given to Roman Catholics, or any other religious denomination, over the rest. Principal Cavan of Toronto has taken a leading part in this movement. Many in Canada are disgusted with the way in which the Church of Rome has not only made the Quebec Government a tool in her hands, but obtained a kind of controlling influence in the Dominion Government also. This last is one of the effects of federation. Now that federation is *un fait accompli*, it would be difficult to undo it. But it is surely very unwise to weaken the bond. I have no idea that Canada as a whole has any desire for union with the United States, although I am told that the younger generation is less opposed to this than their fathers. But it seems a possible thing, if Quebec is to rule the Dominion, that the confederacy will be broken up. And it would be a very serious matter if Ontario were to dissever itself from it. It may seem disloyal even to hint at such a possibility. But the people of Ontario are men of spirit, and cannot abide truckling to the Pope. I cannot help thinking that it is a dangerous experiment that is being tried with them, and one that it would be well not to carry too far.

CHAPTER XIV.

NIAGARA.

FROM Toronto we made a brief detour in order to feast our eyes once more on that grandest, brightest, purest of all earthly spectacles—the Falls of Niagara. I never can express one-tenth part of the emotion to which it gives rise. There is a glory about it which is hardly of the earth earthy. Perhaps it is wisest just to abandon oneself to the luxury of indefinite pleasure. But this is not the way to enable others to share your enjoyment. I will avail myself here of something which I wrote on occasion of a former visit, when I spent three days at Niagara, and at the end seemed to be only learning to spell out the alphabet of its glory.

There is no fine scenery in the neighbourhood. The country round is flat and featureless, and this probably is the cause of the disappointment many visitors feel on their first glimpse of the Falls. Instead of a setting of majestic rocks, with all the glory of Alpine magnificence, the cascade of Niagara is surrounded by level fields and gentle heights, and the only great feature that breaks the monotony is the cliff over which the river is precipitated. The Falls are alone in their magnificence, the one glory of the neighbourhood.

Most people know that a mile or two above the Falls the river Niagara, carrying along the whole body of water collected in Lakes Superior, Huron, Michigan, and Erie, spreads out over an expanse of two or three miles; then it begins to contract, and descends with great velocity, till it rolls over the cliff. Goat Island divides the stream into two just before the plunge. The eastern or American section goes round the island, and descends with great regularity and majesty in a line almost at right angles to the western or Canadian Fall. This other cataract, double the breadth of the former, is borne more rapidly to the edge of the cliff, and comes over it with greater impetuosity. It is in the form of a horseshoe, the curve bending up the stream. In the bosom of the curve there is a chasm in the rock, also passing upwards, causing a tremendous collision between the two masses of water that dash over it on either side. As the Canadian Fall, though not quite so high, is more impetuous than the American, the form of the falling water is more broken, the spray dashes with more vehemence, and the eddies at the bottom are more wild and tumultuous. In the sunshine, when the air is full of vapour, a splendid rainbow spans the fall.

But what is it that gives Niagara such a charm? It is not, as we have remarked, the surrounding scenery. The height is not remarkable—only a hundred and fifty-eight feet on the Canadian side, and a hundred and sixty-four on the American. The Staubbach is five times its height; the Yosemité Fall many times more. What, then, gives Niagara such imperial pre-eminence?

1. In the first place, there is the wonderful *play of life*, extending over the whole length and breadth of the cascade (the breadth of the one fall is one thousand one hundred, and of the other two thousand two hundred feet); the quick, darting movement of the waters, leaping in a marvellous state of exhilaration down the height. This rapidity of motion gratifies and charms one of the most powerful in-

stincts of our nature. For there is nothing that has more attraction for human eyes or more interest for the human mind than the vigorous play of life. Be it the horse racing on the turf, or the rocket flying in the air, or the forked tongue of the lightning, or a ship sliding from a slip into the water, or the express train whirling past us, or the collision of armies, or the collision of intellect in Parliament or Church court—all are attractive because of the display of living energy. Now, about Niagara, everything is instinct with life. Such an immense body of water, estimated at a million and a half tons per minute, flinging itself over more than half a mile of precipices, is a marvellous display of "animated nature." First, there is the preparation for the leap— the gathering of the waters at the "Rapids," a little above the Falls, as if making ready for a tremendous effort. And really, if there were nothing else, the Rapids are a wonderful sight; the water rushes past the "Three Sisters" with such arrowy swiftness that you can hardly follow the wild, perpetual motion. Then, when the edge is reached, there is the unhesitating, fearless plunge, as if the water enjoyed the somersault and did not care one straw for the consequences. If you fix your eye more powerfully on a portion of the waters in their descent, you observe that the desperate earnestness of the great movement is combined with innumerable little touches of frolic and merriment. Every filament of the stream seems to have a life of its own. Everywhere the water is leaping, laughing, dancing, dashing, flying, evidently in the highest spirits. It is as if all the nymphs and naiads of classic story were collected together for some wild frolic, and were entering into it with the keenest enthusiasm. And as fast as one set of naiads plunges into the caldron, there comes another and another in everlasting succession.

2. But while this is your impression as you watch the separate streamlets (as it were), you get a marvellous idea

of majesty when you survey the whole. You are awed by the spectacle of such a vast body of water rolling over, as if in the consciousness of imperial will and resistless might. It is the very emblem of Sovereignty, moving for ever with a force to which any resistance that could be offered would not have the weight of a feather. An unwearied life too, like that of Him who fainteth not, neither is weary.

This idea of pre-eminence and majesty is one of the greatest elements of impression, and grows on you as you give a little scope to your imagination. For all this has been going on hour after hour, year after year, century after century, in daylight and in darkness, in summer and in winter, in war and in peace, if not since the beginning of the world, at least throughout the whole period of history. Where else shall the mind find such a display of the unwearied activity and irresistible will of the Sovereign Creator?

3. Then there is the beautiful display of colour. One of the first things to catch the eye on a sunny day is the bright blue of the water as it curls over the precipice. You see the same shade of blue at the seaside on a sunny day, when the neck of a wave catches the sunbeam, just as it turns over to break. You see also the lily whiteness of the foam; but you do not see at the seaside the pearly lustre of the water as it rushes past you in its fall. Lower down, the water assumes a sea-green colour. Blue, white, green, the waters gleam before you in vast masses of colour; and if it is summer or autumn, you have, in addition, the colours of the surrounding woods and fields, and the azure of the sky above. And if the rainbow sheds its gleam, you have all the colours, and most conspicuous of all the red, which they tell us is never wanting in a perfect picture.

4. Nor must we omit mention of the sound. It is true, many are disappointed with this. They expected a noise of thunder: they find little more than a solemn murmur. But

watch the murmur, and it will gain upon you; it will by-and-by sound like a psalm, like the song of creation to Him who made the heaven and the earth, the sea and the fountains of waters. Then you remember that that psalm has been going up unceasingly from the beginning—before human foot trod the earth, before Red Indian flourished his tomahawk. You try to catch the burden of the psalm: it gives praise to God from everlasting to everlasting. How it contrasts with the broken tribute of our lives, and with our songs of praise so few and so feeble, so little worthy of the great Being, our Creator, Redeemer, Lord, and Father, our Portion, our God for ever!

5. And this leads to yet another view of Niagara—its symbolism. It is a sermon as well as a psalm. Ever since the globe assumed its present form it has been the same. The stream has been flowing on, as we have said, without cessation and without interruption. Could there be a fitter emblem of the grace of God and the love of the Lord Jesus Christ? Could any material thing more fitly portray the endless stream of the divine mercy in Christ, bearing down all opposition and defying all efforts to exhaust it? Does it not seem to echo that beautiful psalm: "Thy mercy, O Lord, is in the heavens; and thy faithfulness reacheth unto the clouds. Thy righteousness is like the great mountains; thy judgments are a great deep: O Lord, thou preservest man and beast. How excellent is thy lovingkindness, O God! therefore the children of men put their trust under the shadow of thy wings. They shall be abundantly satisfied with the fatness of thy house; and thou shalt make them drink of the river of thy pleasures. For with thee is the fountain of life: in thy light we shall see light."

We cannot put up with the impertinences practised on Niagara. The men that trifle with its majesty are not only fools, but impudent knaves. But in this respect things are not so bad as is sometimes represented. On the morning of the day when we reached Niagara, we had read in a Toronto newspaper an elaborate account of a wonderful feat said to have taken place the day before: how a certain American cooper had got into a barrel which he had contrived for the purpose, and being duly strapped inside of it, and the barrel well secured with two padlocks, had been thrown into the river, and after an hour carried over the precipice; how the barrel came to land, and being opened by a friend, the cooper was found to be stunned, but after a copious draught of whisky came all right, and proceeded quietly to his home! Strolling along the Queen Victoria Park, we came on a park-keeper, and on being asked how much truth there was in the paragraph, he simply stared and said, "Not one word." And the landlord of the Clifton corroborated! Of course the absurd story went the round of the world, though it was afterwards contradicted. That any one could have believed it is hardly credible; but how it could have got into the columns of a sober Toronto journal passes belief.

CHAPTER XV.

NORTHFIELD AND HOME.

FROM Niagara we struck eastwards for a few days' visit to Mr. D. L. Moody, who was taking a kind of holiday at Northfield. Northfield, in the west of Massachusetts, is Mr. Moody's birthplace; a quiet New England village, very beautifully situated, commanding a fine view of the Connecticut River and Valley and the mountains beyond. I call it a village, speaking in the English fashion, but in America it is a town, or rather a township. It is seven miles in length; that is to say, there are houses dotted over seven miles, mostly embosomed in trees, and with the appearance of a sparse city suburb. About a mile from what may be called the centre of the town is a plain but bright-looking wooden house, with its screen of fine maple trees in front—the summer home of the great evangelist. A little higher is a smaller and plainer house—Moody's birthplace and the residence of his old mother. When I was last here, nine years before, there had been built by Mr. Moody, a few hundred yards from his house, a large college, with accommodation for some sixty girls. It was designed for the teaching and training of young women, so as to fit them for situations of usefulness—as teachers, missionaries, or otherwise. That was the day of small things; the change from then to now is enormous. Instead of one, there are now five large buildings and six or seven smaller; a fine park of some two hundred acres has been acquired, and its well-kept lawns and undulating surface dotted with trees make it a charming *campus* for the academical buildings scattered over it. Instead of sixty, there are now three hundred young ladies. And four miles away, on the other side of the Connecticut River, is a similar college for young men. A similar group of buildings, large and small, provides accommodation for three hundred. It happened that while we were there the pupils had just assembled for the work of the session. These buildings represented an outlay of about a million dollars, a large part of which arose from royalties on the sale of hymn-books. Mr. Moody was engaged in a great effort to raise a capital sum, the income of which would provide for the expenditure of the two colleges. And being one of those men who do not begin what they do not see their way to finish, he will doubtless, at no distant period, succeed in obtaining his desire.

Mr. Moody, we cannot help thinking, has followed a sound policy in having his colleges separate, each for a single sex. There are many questions at the present day about the higher education in America, both of men and women, and one of these is, whether it is right to allow both sexes to study together at the same college, and to be members of the same classes. For our part, we have a decided conviction that it is not. Anything that tends to obliterate the distinctive qualities of the sexes must be injurious. We cannot but think that this evil result must take place when they study in the same rooms and hear the same lectures—medical lectures, it may be, on subjects of delicacy. We conceive, therefore, that in separating the two schools, Mr. Moody has not only done right, but set a good example to his countrymen.

The colleges are conducted on the principle of self-help. Each student pays a sum of money, but not the whole sum expended on him. In the male college every youth has to give two hours' labour on the farm. In the college for girls there are no servants; the work of the house is done by the young women themselves.

Mr. Moody differs from nearly all the evangelists we have known in his intense concern for the permanent outcome of his labours, and his most careful endeavour to prevent the spirit kindled at his meetings from evaporating in temporary excitement. These colleges are one proof of his desire to build up, to establish Christian habits of life, to set young men and young women to work that will exercise and develop and strengthen feelings that might otherwise be fitful and evanescent. And the great aggressive enterprise with which he is now grappling in Chicago is another evidence of his love of complete and solid work. He is training an agency for going out to the highways and the hedges, for pervading all of Chicago that is neglecting the things that pertain to its peace, and constraining such to come in that the house may be filled. With all his evangelistic ardour, Mr. Moody has no sympathy with fanaticism. His singular Christian shrewdness gives a wide berth to fads.

At Northfield Mr. Moody takes his holiday. The fashion of it is rather peculiar. I asked the man that takes charge of his horses how often they were out. Sometimes, he said, he will require a conveyance at five in the morning, and two or three times during the day, and perhaps till late at night. He would be out before breakfast to confer with workmen about something needed for the schools. The forenoon would be occupied in answering a great correspondence and despatching letters with reference to his engagements and his institutions. In the afternoon, perhaps, he would be acting the peacemaker at some parish meeting, trying to settle an angry quarrel about a public road that threatened a bitter law plea. In the evening he would be away to

Mount Hermon to preach to "the boys." On the Sunday, he would preach in the church which he has built partly for his schools and partly for the neighbourhood, gathering a great congregation round him. In the intervals of employment he would be bright, cheerful, full of fun. He is now the great man of the place, yet is as neighbourly and unaffected and brotherly as in the days when he was a school-boy or a worker on his mother's farm. Nor does he seem a whit more elated by the marvellous influence he has acquired the world over, and the blessed work he has done. Only an instrument in other hands. No man would sing more heartily the 115th Psalm, or more cordially take for his motto, *Laus Deo*.

We are yet more than three thousand miles from home; but I am tired writing, and "it is fit the spell should break of this protracted dream." From Northfield to New York we had a peep of New England, particularly Northampton, Hartford, and Newhaven, much regretting that we were obliged this time to pass over the great cradle of the American republic. At New York we tarried but a day. There had been rain for a week, and there was rain still, and the newspapers were having leaders, "Will it ever stop?" Worse than that, there had been a terrific storm at sea, and the coast-line of New York State had been fearfully injured. It was a gruesome prospect to take to the sea in such weather; but, much to our satisfaction, we learned that the storm had been confined to the shore, and did not extend to the ocean. On a Saturday morning we got on board our old ship the *Furnessia*, and were met by a warm and excellent friend, General Swayne, whose acquaintance we had made in the train between Victoria and Winnipeg, who presented us with a charming basket of fruit, and a bundle of illustrated journals and magazines, to refresh mind and body by the way. Half an hour after leaving New York we were involved in mist; we had to cast anchor in the bay, and did not get it lifted for forty-eight hours; but when we did get off we pegged steadily away. At last the welcome shores of old Ireland greeted us, and by-and-by the Mull of Cantire and the green fields and white cottages of Arran. On a gloomy forenoon we sailed up the Clyde all the way to Glasgow. The first thing that caught my eye was a placard—"The late Dr. Somerville." So he, too, had gone where we should see his beaming face no more.

At last we found ourselves at home, and with nothing but good news awaiting us. We had gone out under the shadow of the psalm, "I will lift up mine eyes unto the hills." We now, after traversing fifteen thousand miles, returned with a new sense of its reality, and with a new interest in the question, "What shall I render to the Lord for all his benefits towards me?"

APPENDIX.

PROHIBITION IN THE UNITED STATES.

I HAVE said that one of the objects I had in view in my visit to America was to get authentic information on the working of prohibition, and the regulation of the drink traffic generally. I will put down in this Appendix the chief results of my inquiries, although they are yet somewhat imperfect.

But, first, I must refer to a document which I consider to be of no little value, in virtue of the source from which it comes. It is entitled "Report on Liquor Traffic Legislation in the United States, issued during the recess, and presented to both Houses of Parliament, by command of Her Majesty. London, 1888." This report, requested no doubt by the Marquis of Salisbury, is forwarded to him by Sir L. S. Sackville West, our Minister at Washington, and bears to have been drafted by Mr. Edwardes, the Secretary of Legation. Mr. Edwardes obtained very full information from her Majesty's consuls in the United States, and, as Sir L. West remarks, the report is very interesting, and has been compiled with great care. In several instances an opinion is expressed as to the working of the liquor laws of the several states, and Mr. Edwardes says that these opinions "are those of persons occupying high positions, the duties of which give them due opportunities of being earnest and impartial judges on this all-important subject." In these circumstances the judgment so expressed may well be accepted by the people of this country as trustworthy and conclusive. I will extract so much as will show the state of the case in the states where prohibition has been the law in whole or in part.

MAINE (population, 648,936).—"The manufacture, sale, and keeping for sale, of intoxicating liquors are forbidden in Maine by a law passed in 1851, and by the Constitution of 1884, the Organic Law being amended by the adoption of prohibition in that year by a large majority of the popular vote.

"The results of prohibition in this state are looked upon by prohibitionists as most satisfactory, and there is no movement in favour of a repeal of the law. All breweries and distilleries have been suppressed; the liquor traffic has been reduced to one-twentieth of its former proportions. Grog shops are unknown in smaller towns and villages. It is said that 12,000,000 dollars are saved annually which would have been spent in drink.

"The extension of the industries in this state is attributed by some to prohibition. It is, however, still impossible to suppress entirely the liquor traffic in the larger towns, the penalties for keeping liquor for sale and other offences against the law being insufficient to prevent the traffic from being carried on with profit."

[We commend this report on Maine to the careful study of the Earl of Wemyss. If we mistake not, it was just about the date of the report that his lordship publicly declared that prohibition was a dead letter in Maine, that there was no diminution of drinking, and no benefit but much harm from the Act. Compare this with the statements—"The liquor traffic has been reduced to one-twentieth of its former proportions." "It is said that 12,000,000 dollars are saved annually which would have been spent in drink."]

VERMONT (population, 332,286).—"A prohibitory provision became law in this state in 1852. By it no one can manufacture or sell spirituous liquors, with a very few exceptions. It is generally held that intemperance has decreased in this state since the passing of this Act."

GEORGIA (population, 1,542,180).—"The liquor traffic in this state is regulated by an Act by which each county votes whether liquors shall be sold or not. Elections for this purpose can be held once every three years. Out of 136 counties in the state, 101 have voted in favour of prohibition.

"It is reported that in the counties where prohibition exists, generally known as 'dry' counties, the result has been excellent. High license has been tried in some counties, but the results not having given satisfaction, that system has been abandoned for prohibition.

"It is held that though the revenue has suffered from prohibition in the counties, the opening up of new enterprise, and the general prosperity of the people at large, tend to the belief that a few years under the present system of prohibition will rather add to than diminish the revenue."

ALABAMA (population, 1,262,585).—"In the fourth Congressional District of this state, where prohibition was enacted, the benefits to the population (the negroes being four-fifths of the whole number) have been so great that the former opponents to the law have changed their opinion, and now assist in its enforcement. It is alleged that crime is diminished one-third since the existence of prohibition."

KANSAS (population, 996,096).—"This state passed a prohibition law in 1881, whereby no intoxicating liquors of any kind can be manufactured or sold, exceptions being made as to liquor required for medicinal, scientific, and mechanical purposes. It is held that this law is universally carried out in the state, and is working to great advantage."

IOWA (population, 1,624,615).—"This state passed a prohibition law which took effect on 4th July 1884.... The strict enforcement of this prohibition law has been found to be a matter of great difficulty, nor has it been long enough in force to [enable us to] form any decided opinion of its effect."

RHODE ISLAND (population, 276,531).—After a very full recitation of Acts and forms of procedure, the report concludes :—" This system has naturally caused a great loss to the state from license fees. Statistics, however, show in some towns a decrease of drunkenness and offences chargeable to the intemperate use of intoxicating liquors. The enforcement of this system is most arduous, and there is no doubt but violation and defiance of this prohibition law is carried on to a great extent with impunity."

[The law was repealed in 1889.]

The general result of these reports, if not strongly in favour of prohibition, is at the least so far in favour of it as to show that the contemptuous way in which it has been treated recently both by newspapers and individuals as if it were a failure is altogether unwarranted.

Of all the states in which it has been sought to work prohibition, that which has attracted by far the greatest attention of late is Kansas. It is comparatively a new state, and the prohibitory law was enacted in 1880. The contest was very keen, and the result not very decisive—92,302 for, and 84,304 against. There was no little bitterness and contempt shown after this decision. In February 1881 a prohibitory law was enacted to carry out this decision, which was amended in 1885, and again in 1887. The last amendment was directed against drug shops, some of which had become almost as bad as saloons.

The law is now enforced in Kansas in a very rigorous way. Mr. Maynard in the account of his inquiries which he has published (" The Facts about Kansas," by L. A. Maynard), says that few of the guilty escape, be they rich or poor. One of the first men sent to jail in Topeka for violation of the law was an old citizen who was reputed to be worth 200,000 dollars. The proprietors of two of the leading hotels in Topeka are now in prison for a similar offence. Few "joint-keepers" (as illegal sellers are now called) venture to dispute the law : on one occasion twenty-one out of forty-seven that had been indicted, pleaded guilty, and threw themselves on the mercy of the court. And conviction means not only imprisonment, but often *work upon the rockpile.* The rockpile is a heap of large stones in the yard which prisoners have to break with hammers into road metal.

The testimonies of the highest authorities to the beneficial effects of the prohibition law in this state seem to be beyond challenge. Conspicuous among them are the ex-Governor and the present Governor. The ex-Governor, Mr. John Martin, was at first a determined opponent of the measure. He did not believe in making men sober by Act of Parliament. He had little faith in the morality of a man that did not steal only because the law said he must not (yet he upheld laws against theft). He thought prohibition a piece of grandmotherly legislation. But after seeing its results he became its strenuous defender. In a pamphlet entitled "Prohibition in Kansas : Facts, not Opinions" (a statement prepared by friends of temperance, and "indorsed by Governor Lyman M. Humphrey, the officers of state, and the judges of the Supreme Court of Kansas"), we find the following remarkable extract from Governor Martin's biennial message to the Legislature in January 1887 :—

"Three general elections have been held in Kansas since the adoption of the prohibition amendment to the constitution. At each of these elections the people have reaffirmed their decision against the manufacture or sale of intoxicating liquors as a beverage, by electing Legislatures pledged to the support of the amendment. At the election in November last this question was a paramount issue, and again, by an emphatic majority, the sovereign verdict of the people was pronounced against the saloon.

"A great reform has just been accomplished in Kansas. Intemperance is steadily and surely decreasing. In thousands of homes where want and wretchedness and suffering were once familiar guests, plenty, happiness, and contentment now abide. Thousands of wives and children are better clothed and fed than when the saloons absorbed all the earnings of husbands and fathers. The marvellous material growth of the state during the past six years has been accompanied by an equally marvellous moral progress, and it can be fairly and truthfully asserted than in no portion of the civilized world can a million and a half of people be found who are more temperate than are the people of Kansas."

The present Governor (Humphrey) said in his message to the Legislature, January 1889:—"The growth of public sentiment in support of constitutional prohibition in Kansas is steady, healthy, and unmistakable. In the last campaign no political party had the temerity to demand a resubmission of the question to the people, in the face of a popular verdict that has been repeated and emphasized every time the popular sense has been taken. As an issue in Kansas politics, resubmission is as dead as slavery. The saloon as a factor in politics, as a moral iniquity, has been outlawed and made a fugitive and a vagabond on the face of the earth, or that part of it within the territorial limits of Kansas."

As another illustration of the striking change which experience has caused in the views of former keen opponents, the following extract from a speech of Senator P. G. Lowe, delivered at Leavenworth, Kansas, March 30, 1889, is very interesting:—" I opposed prohibition because I believed it not the best way to deal with the evils of intemperance. I voted against the prohibitory amendment. In the state Senate I advocated resubmission, firmly believing that the people ought to have an opportunity to again vote upon that question. But my ideas were overruled by the Legislature, and laws enacted to enforce prohibition. And now prohibition is the fixed and unalterable law of the state. There is more than 100,000 majority in favour of it. Since the prohibitory amendment went in with a majority in favour of it, the state has gained 700,000 people, and it is a fact that an overwhelming majority came to Kansas because of the prohibitory law. The sentiment is growing stronger every day. ......People who oppose it are becoming more and more reconciled every day. Hundreds of men who believed this law would prove impracticable, and work more evil than good, would not now vote for an open saloon for anything, and I am one of them. I have come to the conclusion that saloons are not a necessary evil, and no vote of mine will ever encourage the opening of one. I believe it to be the moral and religious duty of all good citizens of this city to lend their moral and substantial support to the police commissioners in enforcing this and every other law. It is the law of the land, made by a majority of our people, and the sooner we, as a whole and united people, support the authorities in its enforcement, the sooner the demagogues and disturbers will be out of the business. I make no apologies for this speech. I speak from experience and conviction, and from my heart."

We turn to Mr. Maynard again for testimonies as to the effect of the new law on material and moral interests. Describing Fort Scott as having been notorious for lawlessness and immorality, he says:—" In 1875, when the city had about one-third its present population, there were two hundred and twenty-three arrests for drunkenness, and three hundred and thirty-seven other charges. In 1887, the population having risen from five thousand to fifteen thousand, there were one hundred and sixteen arrests for drunkenness, and two hundred and eighty-two for other charges. The fees of the police judge have fallen from two thousand four hundred dollars a year to eight hundred. The police force has been reduced from nine to five. The county jail has but five prisoners. The reputation of Fort Scott for law, order, and public morality is now as good as that of any other city of its size in the land, and much better than most of those in saloon states. Its streets are safe at any time of night, and the midnight carousal and drunken brawl are things of the past."

Here is a galaxy of testimonies. Judge Dewey of Abilene says: "No prisoners at present in the county jail." Judge Strang of Larned: "Our jails are empty." The attorney of Clay County: "Crime in this county has decreased three-fourths." Judge Pipher of Manhattan: "There has been a wonderful decrease of crime in this city." Mr. Sheafor of Concordia, County Cloud: "Crime in this county is almost unknown, and our jail is empty most of the time." Mr. Sarviss of Clifton: "Crime has decreased at least forty per cent." Warden Smith of the State Penitentiary: "The number of inmates has fallen off over one hundred in the past eighteen months, and I attribute this to the prohibitory law."

Statistics in abundance might be quoted as to the effects on the churches and schools of the state. We prefer to note a statement as to prostitution, and one or two notices of an improved domestic condition:—

"In such cities as Fort Scott and Topeka (the capital) I was told that since the saloons and dance-houses had been closed, immoral women had almost entirely disappeared from the streets. A prominent clergyman and old resident of Leavenworth told me that in the former days there were many portions of that city where no respectable person would be seen after nightfall. They were full of dance-houses, gambling-dens, and houses of ill repute, and vice was bold and rampant" ("Facts about Kansas," page 30).

As to improved homes: A common labourer visited one of the general stores of Atchison, just before last Christmas time, to buy some toys for his children. He had been a drinking man, and his purse was usually very light when it came to buying anything for his family. But on this occasion he insisted on buying liberally, for he said, " I want you to understand that I am taking better care of my boys and girls than I did when the saloons had a hold of me."

A *habitué* of the saloons of Topeka found that after the saloons were shut up he was able to save six dollars a month more than formerly. This amount he handed to his wife at the end of the first month, saying, " There, take that, and get yourself something with it; that's extra money." His explanation was, " I made it out of prohibition."

A drinking man, after prohibition passed, had to send for his drink to some place at a considerable distance, and buy it in large quantities, or do without. One day, when he came to town, he found he had just three dollars—the price of a case of liquor. He had promised his little daughter a pair of new shoes, which he could not get if he went in for the liquor. " If it has come to this," he said, " I will let the liquor go. My little girl shall have her shoes." This was the last of the liquor trade with this man. The shoes did the business for him, he said.

We conclude our testimonies from Kansas with that of the Rev. H. Grattan Guinness of London:—" Kansas is a marvel—roomy, bright, sunny, Christian, with no drink traffic, no drunkards, no drunkards' wives, no drunkards' children, empty jails, and no pauperism."

There is yet another aspect of the prohibition question on which we must try to throw some light—the recent vote against it in Rhode Island, Massachusetts, Pennsylvania, West Virginia, and New Hampshire. I believe that that vote has been very much misunderstood in this country, and that if the whole circumstances were known, the conclusion to be come to would be very unlike that which has been expressed by some in all the confidence of ignorance.

Let us take the case of Massachusetts. We in this country are prone to suppose that the vote there lay between prohibition and such an iron-bound system of licensing as we have in this unfortunate country. Very much the reverse. For long Massachusetts has had a law which confers local option on the towns and counties. Many other states have a similar law. And in Massachusetts, under the influence of local option, the sale of drink has been prohibited in many parts of the state. And the recent contest was in effect a contest between local option and universal prohibition. Many of the friends of temperance believed that more good could be done at present under local option than under universal prohibition. They saw the difficulty of enforcing prohibition in such a city as Boston. They deemed it unwise to try what could not be carried into effect. The whole matter is explained in the subjoined extract from an address by Rev. Dr. Cuyler of Brooklyn :—

"A certain number of people, and good people, were not prepared to touch the constitution of the old commonwealth, and they said, 'If there be temperance legislation, put it on the statute book and not in the constitution.' That carried a certain number of temperance men undoubtedly. Then again there were large numbers of temperance towns now living and working under local option that have shut up every dram-shop, who felt that they were to gain nothing, perhaps, by the constitutional amendment, and felt there might be some risk of losing what they had gained; at any rate, in good faith, according to their judgment, they voted against the amendment. Why, Cambridge, that refused to license a single rum-den, gave two thousand against our amendment. The highly-cultured religious town of Newton, that generally votes a thousand against license, and has not an open rum-shop in it, gave five hundred majority against the amendment. Brother Moody's own town of Northfield gave nearly a hundred majority against the amendment. Why? Because those people were in favour of rum? No; but according to their way of looking at it, they thought it was better to leave things as they were. I am not saying they are right or wrong, but I do stand up for this, that the verdict of the people of Massachusetts is not to be construed in favour of the unrestricted license and sale of intoxicants. Nor is it the victory of the dram-shop that a great many people over the land mistakenly imagine; for be it observed that the forces of temperance were divided and the saloon powers were united."

I can fully corroborate what Dr. Cuyler says of Northfield. While there, I never saw a vestige of a drink-shop in it, and a more orderly or industrious community it would not be easy to find.

Then with regard to Pennsylvania. That great state has quite recently begun to try the system of high license. Many of the friends of temperance judged it unwise to press for prohibition until they should have time to make a proper trial of the other system. It was known that under high license hundreds of the lower class of saloons had succumbed and passed away. It seemed of very doubtful expediency to set this method aside so soon, and adopt one which in such a city as Philadelphia all experience showed it would be very difficult to work. In these circumstances the adverse vote on the question of prohibition need surprise no one; the wonder rather is that its friends should have mustered so strong.

Many excellent friends of temperance prefer the high-license plan, as being more practicable than prohibition. The great Catholic Congress at Baltimore supported it very cordially, and obtained for this the thanks of the highly Protestant and evangelical *New York Observer*.

In the body of this little book references will be found to Long Beach and Pasádena in Southern California, and to the North-West Territories and Manitoba in Canada.

The sum of the whole matter seems to be—

1. That if every one would agree to prohibition, it would be a vast benefit, would sweep away unnumbered evils, and bring to a community no ordinary measure of peace and prosperity.

2. That where all do not agree, prohibition to be successful needs two things—(1) the hearty support of the majority, and (2) energetic measures to enforce it on the part of the magistrates, police authorities, and other persons of influence.

3. That the chief difficulty in the way of prohibition is in large cities and old states, where the drink interest is strong, and where drinking-habits have been almost inextricably mixed up with the social life of the community. It is here that high license finds its chief advocates.

4. That its best prospect is in comparatively new localities, or sparsely-peopled districts.

It will be of singular benefit to have the problem worked out more fully in such states as Kansas, Iowa, and Maine. If such happy results as those already found in Kansas should be fully confirmed, and the state should be seen to enjoy quite an exceptional prosperity, others might be persuaded to follow her example, and even the old citadels, now so inveterate in their resistance, might be constrained to yield.

THE END.

www.ingramcontent.com/pod-product-compliance
Lightning Source LLC
Chambersburg PA
CBHW030312170426
43202CB00009B/974